GW00891352

"You can forget about Tom Peters and Jim Collins. Screw Jack Welch. They're all dinosaurs. If you want truly innovative, revolutionary ideas to make your company happier and more successful then Will McInnes is your man and *Culture Shock* is the book you need to read.

I've admired Will's vision of a better way to do business and his courage to actually follow through and do it for years. I've also been green with envy over the cool culture and stellar results he's championed at Nixon McInnes and this excellent book shows you exactly how you can do it yourself."
Alex Kjerulf, Chief Happiness Officer, Woohoo Inc.

"A provocative and inspiring work that serves as a call to arms for all of us – yes ALL of us – to take responsibility and make the changes now that will make the world of work and beyond a better place. The time is past for the old external shareholder models of commerce and the push is on to find sounder, more meaningful ways of doing business. *Culture Shock* is a fun to read manual for this new world, providing sage advice and pragmatic examples of how businesses do it differently, producing better results for their employees, customers and community. Spread the love – buy five and give four away to random business contacts."
Carole Leslie, Policy Director, Employee Ownership Association

"The world of work is changing, and changing in very fundamental ways. We are just at the start of a period of significant disruption, partly driven by the internet, partly driven by the collapse into irrelevance of old ways of working, and partly driven by the changing expectations of the workforce. This is going to be longer and more significant period of change than most realize and we will need stories to help us make sense of what is happening. Will

McInnes helps us to start thinking what these sense making stories might be and we would do well to listen."
Euan Semple, consultant and author of *Organizations Don't Tweet, People Do*

"Our global economy desperately needs more alternatives to the conventional corporate model. If you're starting a business or are already running one, it's important to know that you DO have other options and that you DON'T have to follow the conventional norm. Will's book provides us with encouragement, inspiration, and examples for the endless possibilities of doing business in a different, better, and healthier way."
Blake Jones, President & CEO, Namasté Solar, USA

"Will McInnes has taken a subtle tack in *Culture Shock*, asking deceptively direct questions about the nature of the workplace that are secretly subversive, and introducing us to successful and inspiring companies that are more open and democratic than many will think possible."
Stowe Boyd, author and social tools researcher

"Will McInnes has nailed it, and just when we needed it most. Inspiring and comprehensive, *Culture Shock* is aspirational future thinking with its feet firmly on the ground."
Jemima Kiss, Digital Media correspondent, *The Guardian*

"This book is the field notes of a pioneer. In it, you'll find the distilled insight of a man whose persistent pursuit of the open path is matched only by his robust positivity. May it guide you well."
Dan McQuillan, Lecturer in Creative and Social Computing at Goldsmiths, University of London, and co-founder of Social Innovation Camp

CULTURE SHOCK

A HANDBOOK
FOR 21ST CENTURY BUSINESS

Will McInnes

A John Wiley & Sons, Ltd., Publication

This edition first published 2012
© 2012 Will McInnes

Registered office
John Wiley & Sons Ltd, The Atrium, Southern Gate, Chichester, West Sussex,
PO19 8SQ, United Kingdom

For details of our global editorial offices, for customer services and for
information about how to apply for permission to reuse the copyright material
in this book please see our website at www.wiley.com.

The right of the author to be identified as the author of this work has been
asserted in accordance with the Copyright, Designs and Patents Act 1988.

Wiley publishes in a variety of print and electronic formats and by print-on-
demand. Some material included with standard print versions of this book may
not be included in e-books or in print-on-demand. If this book refers to media
such as a CD or DVD that is not included in the version you purchased, you
may download this material at http://booksupport.wiley.com. For more
information about Wiley products, visit www.wiley.com.

Designations used by companies to distinguish their products are often claimed
as trademarks. All brand names and product names used in this book are trade
names, service marks, trademarks or registered trademarks of their respective
owners. The publisher is not associated with any product or vendor mentioned
in this book. This publication is designed to provide accurate and authoritative
information in regard to the subject matter covered. It is sold on the
understanding that the publisher is not engaged in rendering professional
services. If professional advice or other expert assistance is required, the
services of a competent professional should be sought.

Library of Congress Cataloging-in-Publication Data
McInnes, Will.
    Culture shock : a handbook for 21st century business / Will McInnes.
        p. cm.
    Includes index.
    ISBN 978-1-118-31243-8 (cloth)
1. Organizational change.   2. Leadership.   3. Culture shock.   I. Title.
    HD58.8.M3465 2012
    658.4'06–dc23
                                                              2012023632

A catalogue record for this book is available from the British Library.
ISBN 978-1-118-31243-8 (hardback) ISBN 978-1-118-44368-2 (ebk)
ISBN 978-1-118-44372-9 (ebk) ISBN 978-1-118-44373-6 (ebk)

Set in 11 on 16 pt Adobe Jenson Pro by Toppan Best-set Premedia Limited
Printed in Great Britain by TJ International Ltd, Padstow, Cornwall, UK

CONTENTS

FOREWORD

I vividly recall the first time I stepped into the offices of NixonMcInnes in Brighton, England. The walls were bright blue and yellow-green. Sunshine poured in on a floor plan that was open and inviting and the kitchen area had a blackboard wall where people had written pithy notes to each other. But beyond the fun bricks and mortar, there was something different in the atmosphere at NixonMcInnes.

Yes, there was the hum of great people talking about big ideas for some of the coolest clients in the UK – but there was more than that. There was a general feeling of peace in the air that you simply don't feel when you walk inside most angst-laden organizations today. Looking in people's eyes, I saw a spark there. They had been expecting our visit – my colleague Miranda Ash was with me as well – and as we talked over sandwiches and drinks, I got a deeper sense of what made the NixonMcInnes environment so remarkable. It was their steadfast commitment to doing business differently, coupled with an understanding each employee had as to how that enhanced their client work, helped them solve problems, invited them to grow personally and changed the way they engaged with their community that was making the difference.

Put the words "democracy" and "workplace" together and many people – particularly business leaders – can't envision how that's possible. We generally accept political democracy as the right way to go, but suggest applying it to the business world and eyebrows go up. We've been entrenched in command and control behaviors for too long to see another way. Most businesses look and behave just like businesses did in the 1950s!

However, this pattern is shifting. A new wave of disruptive organizations – many featured in the following chapters – are doing business differently. Change in the workplace isn't some far-off prophecy – indeed, for the past 15 years I've had a front-row seat watching the rising trends towards purpose before profits, towards more enlightened leadership, organizational democracy, and the intelligent use of technology to help people collaborate and move faster. Now is the time for change.

In 1997, I founded a membership and certification organization called WorldBlu, which is now the largest global network of organizations committed to democracy in the workplace. We have over a quarter of a million members in nearly 80 countries worldwide. WorldBlu-certified democratic workplaces include some of the most well-respected brands in the world – Zappos, the WD-40 Company, DaVita, HCL Technologies and NixonMcInnes.

My goal is to see one billion people working in free and democratic workplaces. NixonMcInnes is one of those organizations contributing to this goal, and Culture Shock will show you how to join the movement and start building your own progressive workplace. I hope you will enjoy this forward-thinking, action-packed and remarkably creative book by Will McInnes, co-founder and Managing Director of NixonMcInnes. I know I did.

Traci Fenton
Founder and CEO, WorldBlu
2012

INTRODUCTION

'Another world is not only possible, she is on her way. On a quiet day, if you listen carefully, you can hear her breathing.'

Arundhati Roy

People say business is broken. You know what? I agree. Screw how that kind of business is: the 20th century rapacious school of business that ruined its people, corrupted its environment and lumbered like an eyeless, earless giant from room to room, smashing plates, breaking doors down and filling its pockets with gold coins. We've had enough. We, the people. We, the workers, the shareholders, the managers, the community members, the entrepreneurs and the everyday folk.

So what do we do? Do we give up? Do we throw out everything of business, and patiently wait for some new kind of thing to emerge that can solve the problems that need solving? I cannot.

I cannot leave the future to the lumbering eyeless giants any more than I can leave it to the short-term-ist politicians, or the stretched and challenged not-for-profits. And I cannot patiently wait – the warning lights are blinking urgently, there are problems that cannot be left any longer. And to hate is not enough, because to sit back and criticize business and bonuses and bankers and 'the way things just are' will not make the slightest difference.

What we have to do is to change business. 'We' is you and me, and your colleagues, and mine. And them over there. If we really decide to do this, we can. This is the opportunity of a lifetime.

We have to start operating our businesses in new ways. Because what good business has to give is so, so needed. In this book, we look at the good businesses, the progressive companies who do things differently, the crazy ones.

In this book you will find out how different companies are doing things better, right now. Not theories, but real-world realities. The benefits of these new progressive business practices are substantial and broad – from improved financial measures like lower costs, higher customer lifetime value, through to the less measurable but more meaningful, like providing purpose and satisfaction to people and helping the world become more sustainable.

To help you both learn and then take action we have chapters on Purpose and Meaning, Democracy and Empowerment, Progressive People, Conscious Leadership, Organizational Openness, Change Velocity, Tech DNA and Fair Finances. The first four chapters deal mainly with the human aspects of 21st century business, whilst the next-four chapters deal mainly with the organizational characteristics of 21st century business, although many themes repeat.

As you read, I hope that you will see and then take heart from the knowledge that we are not alone. We are part of something bigger. Our numbers grow! Giant Indian software companies with multi-billion dollar revenues, ripping up business-as-usual management practices. Loosely connected networks of hacktivists, working collaboratively to bring down their common enemy. Fast-growing American solar energy companies, entirely owned by their workforce. Independent, rebellious Scottish brewers, raising funds from their fans.

This is a movement. My hope is that you will join the movement and make a difference in your organization. That is my purpose in this. You. We need you. Come and change the world.

Will McInnes

@willmcinnes
http://www.nixonmcinnes.co.uk/
http://willmcinnes.com/

CHAPTER ONE

PURPOSE AND MEANING

Last century we in the world of business lost sight of higher meaning, of purpose beyond simply profits. People – many of us – went to work every day without a sense of a more meaningful contribution beyond the monthly pay packet, the sense of responsibility, slaving away working for the man, for anonymous, financially-driven shareholders, in businesses large and small. The trudge, the wear and tear of everyday business and the bad behaviour of many corporations turned business into a dirty word.

So what do we do now?

This is the opportunity we have before us: to guide our organizations, our teams, our projects towards higher meaning. To be part of the movement that demands a greater contribution from business than just profits. To discover and share real purpose.

A Purpose of Significance

An organization designed to thrive in this radically different century before us has a very clear purpose, which creates meaning way beyond financial results. A purpose that solves big, meaningful challenges and opportunities in society. Something that really makes sense. This is a Purpose of Significance.

WHY DOES A PURPOSE OF SIGNIFICANCE MATTER?

The simple truth is that, today, the accepted wisdom is that the purpose of a business is to increase shareholder value. Purely and simply. This is what is ingrained in business schools and boardrooms, in the minds of so many of us – it is very hard for any of us to stray from this path.

And, as Peter Drucker said, 'What's measured improves' and, in business, this is what has been measured and has 'improved': the purpose of business has narrowly and determinedly fixed on growing the wealth of its shareholders. Significant to a few, but not to the wider world. Some improvement.

Increasingly, we're realizing that this destination isn't such a pretty place. As the inspiring economist, Umair Haque, tweeted: 'Making shareholder enrichment the basis of an economy is probably an idea that belongs up there with Cheez Whiz and Donald Trump's hair'.

Zooming out, when we look at the macro picture, it is clear to all of us in the Western developed world that we are in an even worse hole. The collective efforts of a whole global economic model based on output, and measured in dollars, euros and pounds, has left the most developed nations with thriving but horribly volatile businesses and a society that is fat, debt-ridden and unhappy. (By the way, these are challenges of real significance; and huge positive business opportunities, if addressed in the right way with the right intentions.)

POLITICIANS AND NORMAL PEOPLE TOO

When politicians, such as former French President Sarkozy and British Prime Minister Cameron, start to look seriously at how to include measurements of happiness in policy, we business people should pay attention. This is a massive change in purpose, an attempt to reinject significance and meaning; and, what's more, led by government who we are used to haranguing for being out of date and late to the party. Wake up, progressive business people!

People are changing too. Whether you call them customers, consumers or citizens, attitudes are shifting. Expectations are changing – think about what you expect from a business, what you demand, and what is actually delivered. What would be amazing?

People like you, whose basic needs have been well met, are increasingly seeking out experiences, services and products with a narrative that is authentic and sustainable; stuff which has provenance. You want great service. You want the basics, done excellently. You want a personal interface to the organization – an ability to get a handle on it when you need to. And, increasingly, you demand a higher-order contribution beyond all of that. See the growth in sales of organic food, the rise of the micro-brewery, the niche bicycle design company, the resistance towards powerful supermarkets in small towns and villages, the Buy Local movement, the gastro pub, the return of the handmade. This is not to say that small is the only way, but it is a powerful clue as to how attitudes and expectations are changing.

In this ultra-competitive business landscape, our organizations desperately need a higher purpose. A story of meaning. A mission that inspires. A cause to get behind and a movement to belong to.

WHY WILL A PURPOSE OF SIGNIFICANCE MAKE A DIFFERENCE?

So what's the prize? What's the impetus that we can use to cajole others? Why should our colleagues pay attention to creating purpose?

In practical terms a clear purpose helps in the following ways:

- Attracting and then retaining the very best talent in your workforce (see Chapter Three, Progressive People).
- Unlocking the highest levels of engagement (also in Chapter Three).
- Acquiring and retaining customers in an environment of ruthless competition and the ever-present threat of commoditization.
- Providing both a compass and a motivation for innovation.
- Gaining competitive advantage from very diverse (and often otherwise disruptive) stakeholders by framing the organization in a context that truly matters and contributes to society.

WHAT DOES A PURPOSE OF SIGNIFICANCE LOOK LIKE?

The idea that Purpose really makes a difference in business is not new. In their excellent work, which led to *Built to Last* and *Good to Great* (a personal favourite), Jim Collins and Jerry Porras established the idea that visionary companies have a Big Hairy Audacious Goal, a 'BHAG' at their core. 'A true BHAG is clear and compelling, serves as a unifying focal point of effort, and acts as a clear catalyst for team spirit.' So the notion of having a big purpose is well-established. It is not new or radical.

Indeed, most CEOs and entrepreneurs know that it is their responsibility to ensure that there is a clear and compelling vision and mission for the organization. Most internal comms teams and brand people have worked good and hard at 'cascading' the big message, and plastered the accompanying values across the headquarter's reception area and on meeting room walls.

So, what is different with this movement of 21st century businesses? How does this differ from the good ol' purpose we used to know and trust in the last century? Today, it is the Significance bit.

We can put a man on the moon, we can invent better mousetraps and sell a bajillion plastic bottles of mineral water. To be 'compelling' in today's world, we must work towards the urgent, the difficult, the pressing problems of our time.

The enlightened shareholders, employees, partners and consumers of the 21st century demand a Purpose of Significance.

A Purpose of Significance: the checklist

Here is how to think about how to design a purpose that fits your organization:

- Does our Purpose address a fundamental problem that is caused or exacerbated by this businesses industry?
- Does our Purpose lead to decisions which can suppress or limit short-term financial gains for longer-term achievements?
- Does our Purpose inspire a community to develop?
- Does our Purpose address a fundamental injustice in the world?
- Does our Purpose disrupt and positively revolutionize a whole marketplace?
- Does our Purpose fundamentally make the world a better place?

This is our job. This is how to make business better. This is how business can help to solve the big problems of our time.

Who is leading the way?

Let's look at some examples of pioneering businesses to get under the skin of what is really possible here.

Patagonia, California, USA
Patagonia, the manufacturer of outdoor equipment with a particular heritage in climbing, is a wonderful business.

You may have read *Let My People Go Surfing* by Patagonia founder Yvon Chouinard (if you haven't, do!). The company has a long track record in zigging when other businesses zag, and having a conscience that goes beyond box ticking. Back in 1985, Patagonia was one of the two original creators of the '1% for the Planet' initiative, a global movement of over a thousand companies that donates 1% of sales to a network of environmental organizations worldwide.

In its most recent and perhaps most inspiring and jaw-dropping move, the company has formed an alliance with eBay to actively promote and encourage existing owners of Patagonia equipment and apparel to sell their stuff in a branded shop within eBay called the Common Threads Initiative. It is actively encouraging potential customers to buy second-hand Patagonia goods. And not just inside eBay: items listed for sale in the Common Threads Initiative are also promoted on the 'Used Clothing & Gear' section on Patagonia.com. In conventional thinking, this is plain STUPID! This will, you'd think, negatively impact short-term profits, limit growth, generally not be a good thing to do.

Businesses in the 20th century went out of their way to encourage as many new sales as possible. But, driven by a higher purpose and with a clear sense of itself and what it stands for, Patagonia intends to address tangibly the issues of global sustainability. This not only focuses on one of the greatest challenges our society faces, but also leads from the front: I recently met with one of Patagonia's biggest competitors and he told me, smiling with admiration, that this move 'changes the game, changes everything'. Brilliant!

This is truly a Purpose of Significance in action. As Chounaird is quoted in a *Business Week* article from 2006: 'Every time we do the right thing, our profits go up'. Smart business; 21st century business.

> Patagonia in 2005: $260 m revenues; 1,250 employees.

NOMA AND THE NEW NORDIC CUISINE, COPENHAGEN, DENMARK

Have you heard of Noma? If you're a foodie the answer is, of course, yes. Noma was ranked as best restaurant in the world by *Restaurant* magazine in 2010 and 2011. Noma isn't in New York City, Tuscany, the hills of Catalunya, Paris, London or Tokyo. Noma – famous for dishes and flavours that celebrate the very best of Nordic/Scandinavian produce – is in Copenhagen, the gorgeous capital of Denmark. When you start to look into the story behind Noma there's a fabulous and inspiring account of how purpose and meaning can fuel incredible achievement, and simultaneously create and empower a whole generation of like-minded changers.

As Claus Meyer, co-owner of Noma, describes on his website: 'Less than 10 months after the opening of our restaurant "noma" November 2003, head chef, manager & partner Rene Redzepi and I took the initiative to organize "The Nordic Cuisine Symposium". The day before the symposium in September 2004, at an 18 hour long work-shop, some of the greatest chefs in our region formulated the New Nordic Kitchen Manifesto. The Nordic Cuisine Movement was born!'

This manifesto is a fantastic example of a group of individuals transcending their own self-interests to put down a marker and describe a Purpose of Significance that inspired and enabled a whole movement. Here's that mani-festo in full:

Manifesto for the New Nordic Kitchen

As Nordic chefs we find that the time has now come for us to create a New Nordic Kitchen, which in virtue of its good taste and special character com-pares favourable with the standard of the greatest kitchens of the world.

The aims of New Nordic Cuisine are:

1 To express the purity, freshness, simplicity and ethics we wish to associate with our region.
2 To reflect the changing of the seasons in the meals we make.
3 To base our cooking on ingredients and produce whose characteristics are particularly excellent in our climates, landscapes and waters.
4 To combine the demand for good taste with modern knowledge of health and well-being.

5 To promote Nordic products and the variety of Nordic producers – and to spread the word about their underlying cultures.

6 To promote animal welfare and a sound production process in our seas, on our farmland and in the wild.

7 To develop potentially new applications of traditional Nordic food products.

8 To combine the best in Nordic cookery and culinary traditions with impulses from abroad.

9 To combine local self-sufficiency with regional sharing of high-quality products.

10 To join forces with consumer representatives, other cooking craftsmen, agriculture, the fishing, food, retail and wholesale industries, researchers, teachers, politicians and authorities on this project for the benefit and advantage of everyone in the Nordic countries.

As you can see for yourself, the manifesto is very simple, but the creation and application of that manifesto, the meaning and energy created from it, has inspired a whole movement. The Nordic Cuisine Movement that Meyer describes goes much further than fancy restaurants for the few. In 2005, the manifesto was adopted by the Nordic Council of Ministers and their extended national development programmes. You can find articles about The New

Nordic Cuisine on Denmark.dk the official website of Denmark, and Meyer himself participates in a long-term food programme with the Danish government and universities to improve food health including around childhood obesity.

In doing so, Noma created and placed itself in a context of higher meaning. A backdrop that could engage and impassion every would-be employee, every diner, every producer and supplier.

Would this have been possible if it was simply one person's drive for greatness? If it was the same old story about a celebrity TV-friendly chef on their way to millionaire-dom? Ask a Dane what the New Nordic Cuisine has done, and they will tell you: helped to restore pride in our national identity; changed our expectations and habits around eating and food; promoted Denmark to the world. This is what can be done with the power of Purpose of Significance – change that affects millions, for the good.

> Noma: two Michelin stars; Best Restaurant in the World, 2010 and 2011, *Restaurant* magazine.

ANONYMOUS, THE INTERNET, EVERYWHERE

Anonymous is an interesting organization. For starters, I'm not sure how we can define or understand it as an organization, and certainly not as a business. Anonymous is usually referred to as 'a loose collective of hackers and activists' or similar. Anonymous is very much of the zeitgeist – at the heart of recent activism (that includes the Occupy movement): digitally networked; apparently decentralized; powerfully branded; and, perhaps most fascinating and relevant here, motivated by a very strong sense of values and justice. In this very changed world, we need to look at the edges and the radicals to understand how all of our organizations are going to have to change.

At the time of writing, Anonymous may have:

- Hacked the Sony Playstation Network, creating huge reputational damage and heavily impacting the share price of Sony.
- Hacked the Iranian government.
- Threatened a Mexican drug cartel.
- Threatened NATO.
- Taken down 40 child porn websites and published the names of 1,500 frequent visitors to one of the largest of these.

It would be easy, thinking with a conventional mindset, to write off Anonymous. What would the old-school business person say? 'Kids, hackers, mindless vandals, people with nothing better to do – lock 'em up!' I think that's missing the point. Anonymous is creating enormously powerful results and, at its core, there is this sense of purpose – as they say themselves: 'We are fighters for internet freedom'.

If we pay attention there is much that conventional business can learn from this unpaid, volunteer network of loosely connected activists. What Anonymous provides the 21st century business person with, is an unexpected and powerful example of the real-world results that can be created when people unite behind a shared Purpose of Significance. And Anonymous achieves all of this in a world where there are record numbers of young people unemployed, where technology is increasingly pervasive and disrupting of the status quo and, as Bill Rhodes, the famous banker puts it, 'new technologies mean that markets move in nano seconds'.

Specifically, how does Anonymous communicate its purpose, its intentions and values? How did Anonymous create these in the first place, or do they just emerge and develop over time? What is it that Anonymous does that allows it to transmit its purpose so clearly to the world with so few conventional resources at its disposal? And, perhaps, what would our organization look like if it were more Anonymous-like?

> Anonymous statistics: unknown!

GOOGLE, CALIFORNIA, USA

What about a big business example, a marquee brand? How about Google – a business led by a set of core principles, a business that refuses to provide short-term guidance to Wall Street and, instead, in their own words: 'Rather than thinking about ways in which we can create short-lived economic gains each quarter, we focus on serving our users and delivering the most relevant information as fast as we can'. This is a strategy that has now led the business to play across internet search, online advertising, mobile, book publishing, communications . . . the list goes on and on.

There is, and always has been, a higher purpose to Google's work and for me it is captured in their mantra: 'Organize the world's information and make it universally accessible and useful'. When you look at pretty much everything the company does, that purpose is apparent, is visible and is gluing the whole empire together.

If I am an engineer at Google, I can get excited about unlocking information that isn't yet accessible to those that would benefit from it. If I am a marketer at Google, I can draw on huge and 'free' goodwill in society because the products and services that I need – to address fundamental problems and provide their users with vast value – are there (and often, at no cost because someone else is paying – usually an advertiser). If I am a senior manager, I can excite my people with their contribution to something that goes beyond just earning the next month's pay packet. There is meaning in 'Organizing the world's information', and it is simple enough and clear enough that it can be applied in a whole range of different scenarios, markets and user needs.

What is it about Google's purpose that is significant in the context of this book? First and foremost, Google has made the world better for us all in providing a search engine that connects us to the information we wish to find. This alone is a huge and immeasurable contribution to the world. Google has also disrupted and revolutionized online advertising by developing not only a results-focused model, but also one that rewards merit and always seeks to provide the best result to the user, the searcher. You cannot – in conventional terms – pay Google to get to the top of Google's results (there's a separate industry for that!). It has also democratized online advertising by providing an advertising platform and 'back-end' that from early on allowed 'mom and pop' businesses to quickly and easily promote their business in listings and – with smart, well executed strategies – compete and jostle with the big boys and girls in a given market. And, finally, as described above, Google has provided a role model by showing that a business can generate substantial financial results without bending to the specific and short-term demands of Wall Street.

> Google: $37.9 bn revenue and $9.7 bn profits in 2011 (unaudited); 32,000 employees.

Apple, California, USA

You won't be surprised to see Apple and Steve Jobs mentioned here (indeed, there should be some kind of charitable foundation to which every consultant, speaker, writer and manager must donate when citing Apple as an example of anything remotely good, the company has become such a commonly used case study!). Nevertheless, as Ben Heineman wrote on the *Harvard Business Review* blog network, Jobs didn't run Apple for the gain of shareholders first and foremost: 'in my view, there can also be no question that Jobs was not focused on shareholders or taking short-cuts or short-term actions to maximize shareholder value. Apple has paid no dividends since 1995. It hasn't used leverage. It holds $76 billion in cash with nary a thought of a buy-back. It is hard to argue that fundamental business decisions were driven by stock options (although there is the issue of options back-dating in the debit column).' And yet at the time of writing Apple is swapping positions with Exxon from day to day as the publicly traded company with the largest market capitalization in the world.

What Apple did was create incredible shareholder value as a byproduct of a different and higher purpose – to delight customers, to innovate its way to success – to put, in Jobs' words, a 'ding in the universe'.

You'd think this was obvious and more widely accepted, but it is still considered newsworthy for senior management of global businesses to put such a view forward. As Joe Garner, the Deputy Chief Executive of HSBC UK, recently put it: 'I believe that increasing customer satisfaction will increase profitability'. He's right in my opinion and I applaud him for saying so. But this is news?

And in the new guard we are and will continue to see a massive growth in the number and impact of entrepreneurs that act with broader purpose. As Danna Greenberg, Kate McKone-Sweet, H. James Wilson describe in their book *The New Entrepreneurial Leader: Developing Leaders Who Shape Social and Economic Opportunity*: 'by considering the purpose in both societal and business terms, entrepreneurial leaders scrutinize the common assumption that maximizing shareholder wealth will maximize value for the society at large over time.'

> Apple: $108 bn revenue and $26 bn profits in 2011; 60,400 employees.

GRAMEEN, DHAKA, BANGLADESH

Grameen Bank lends to millions in poverty – mainly women. Grameen Phone is the largest mobile phone provider in Bangladesh with more than 32 million subscribers at the time of writing. Grameen Danone is a joint venture social enterprise providing nutritious yoghurt to children in rural Bangladesh. These are just three of the many Grameen endeavours.

Grameen, right from its start, has been an organization that creates businesses with real purpose, grounded in the gritty realities of the developing world, and creates meaning and results that transform the lives of the people they touch. An unstoppable force. Specifically, Grameen businesses seek to address the following problems in society:

■ Women not having access to or control of finance.
■ Communities not being resilient and self-sufficient.
■ Communities not having access to healthy nutrition.

The brilliant founder of Grameen, and Noble prize winner, Muhammad Yunus, has shown the whole world what is possible when business-minded organizations apply themselves to messy, gritty problems in the developing world.

Grameen Bank: $1.5 bn total assets in 2010; 22,149 employees in 2011.

How can you locate a Purpose of Significance?

Let's get practical. Put simply, there are three steps in the journey towards uniting a group of people in an organization behind a shared purpose:

1 Finding it
2 Framing it
3 Living it.

1 Finding it

Clearly the first step is to find and agree on a purpose that makes sense to the organization and its competencies and can excite and inspire its people. There are two obvious routes to locating a Purpose of Significance:

- from the individual – commonly a leader's personal passion or perspective, and
- from the group – through a collective effort.

In the individual mode, inspiring characters like Muhammad Yunus of Grameen or Yvon Chouinard of Patagonia stumble upon, or are already driven by, a cause or personal mission. We all have passions burning inside us. Locating our own can feel impossible, it can seem so foggy and far from beliefs about what work is and should be. But the happiest and most successful people are generally doing something they love – they love their work *and* they get paid to do it.

Discovering your personal passion and purpose can be as simple as reflecting on what it is you really enjoy, what it is you want to give, what gets you riled, furious, hysterical and arm-waving, laughing out loud. It's about locating those embers that are already burning.

Coaching

The coaching world is very good at this, and there are some great 'visioning' exercises that an experienced coach can take you through. In fact, helping someone find their higher purpose is what gets most coaches excited and passionate. The process is enjoyable, relaxed, enlightening and the results can be life-changing. I myself have worked with the Coaches Training Institute (CTI) and found the quality of their coaches (and their coach training) to be excellent.

- *What's Your Purpose?* (Richard Jacobs): This brilliantly designed work takes you through seven questions to 'Find Your Answer'. I discovered that the audio book was an excellent way of consuming the content and working through the simple, enjoyable exercises. I can still remember how, through the course of a one hour train journey from Brighton to London in the middle of a frazzled busy working day, I sketched out some profoundly useful descriptions of what I wanted to do in the world. Highly recommended.

■ *Leadership: Plain and Simple* (Steve Radcliffe): In this excellent and very easy to read book on leadership, Steve Radcliffe walks you through a very practical approach to locating your own passions and then bringing others on the journey through his Future, Engage, Deliver model. As with *What's Your Purpose?*, there are a really tight set of wonderfully simple, open questions to get you clear, but matched also with practical approaches to getting a wider team performing too.

IN GROUPS

In larger groups, the challenge to find a uniting purpose can feel much harder, but the result is obviously that much more powerful when it engages a whole group – be that a team, a small business, a division or an entire corporation.

My feeling is that, again, the purpose is lingering in the background, waiting to be dusted off and shared around. However hard or poor things have been, teams and organizations are often drawn together by implicit values and a purpose that may be shared but is often buried.

One method for locating a Purpose of Significance here is to run workshop groups of 8 to 15 people in a reasonably quiet and 'safe' space away from normal desks and interruptions and to ask some of the same questions covered in the two books mentioned above, but in a group setting.

In my team, working for our clients (or, equally to develop our own company), we often use white walls and

Post-It notes, or stick index cards up so that everyone can see them, providing prompts like:

- What do we care about?
- Why do we do the work we do?
- What really matters?
- What is the purpose of our organization?
- What do we want for the future of this group/team?
- What can we give that really matters to the world?

You can use the initial surge of answers as the start of a collective discussion about what the shared purpose will be.

For more on doing this at scale, particularly if you are working in a very large organization, there is some excellent information available about the transformation of the American kidney care company DaVita in the Further Reading section at the end of this chapter.

2 FRAMING IT

Having identified a purpose, the vital key over the course of this century is clearly linking this purpose to a matter of significance in the world. For example, whilst working in Denmark, I was told the story of a Danish company called Groundfos – a company with a long history of manufacturing excellent pumps for a variety of purposes, producing some 16 million pump units a year. My friend told me that what Groundfos had done in recent times, to help lift and guide the whole business, was to reframe its matter-of-fact production of pumps in the context of a world where to

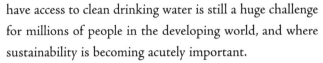

have access to clean drinking water is still a huge challenge for millions of people in the developing world, and where sustainability is becoming acutely important.

Today Groundfos frames what it does in this context: 'Grundfos is a global leader in advanced pump solutions and a trendsetter in water technology. We contribute to global sustainability by pioneering technologies that improve quality of life for people and care for the planet.'

So, the opportunity here is to link what your company does with something that really, really matters in the 21st century.

Find answers to questions like these:

- How does your Purpose link to really significant, worthwhile issues, challenges and needs in the world?
- How clear and alive are those issues in the minds of your people?

3 LIVING IT

Living the Purpose of Significance is the fun bit. It's the bit that, having clarified it, will get easier and more exciting with every day that passes.

It challenges you and those around you to find the link between the work and the purpose.

Living it also means sharing it. This generation of radical businesses is happy to champion and evangelize the issues that they stand for. They share knowledge freely, from seminars to articles and speeches – spreading and championing their cause.

- What can your organization do to champion these significant issues that need fixing in the world?
- How can you share your organization's Purpose of Significance with others?
- Can you create something like the Nordic Cuisine Movement or the 1% for the Planet initiative?
- Who should your organization be collaborating with to see this through?

SUMMARY

This chapter comes first for a reason: it is where everything starts. Engaging with a Purpose of Significance transcends and influences everything else that follows. It is the key to kingdom, the guiding star, the secret sauce! Without a clear, personal and organizational purpose that really matters – a Purpose of Significance – everything else is window dressing and 'nice to have'.

And although it may feel overwhelming and impossible to change, it really is not. Go for it, start soon. You'll amaze yourself and the people around you.

In this chapter on purpose and meaning we have explored the 'why' of your organization. In the next critical chapter, 'Democracy and Empowerment', we look at a core aspect of the 'how' of your organization: Is it just another business, but with a much more meaningful purpose now? Does it act like the millions of everyday organizations in its practices and decision making, or is it also progressive and exciting in the way it gets work done?

FURTHER READING

■ Watch Claus Meyer's talk at Rebuild 21 here – http://bit.ly/cltrshk1 (28 passionate, interesting and amusing minutes)
■ DaVita case studies from *Harvard Business Review* (small fee payable):

  ■ http://Kent Thiry, Mayor of DaVita (bit.ly/cltrshk2)
  ■ http://Kent Thiry; Leadership challenges in building and growing a great company (bit.ly/cltrshk3)

CHAPTER TWO

DEMOCRACY AND EMPOWERMENT

Having explored Purpose and Meaning, and particularly how to locate your personal and organizational purpose, this chapter helps you make that revitalized mission happen in an evolved, exciting way. If the Purpose is the heart, then Democracy and Empowerment are the muscles and the lungs; they make it all real, generating the results in an equally progressive, renewed way. This chapter is about how the organization behaves.

How do businesses typically behave today? Taking a step back it looks like most businesses are modeled on, and behave in, the military paradigm of top-down, command and control. But that is simply too slow and too stupid for the 21st century – the military themselves agree with that.

This post-industrial world is markedly different, and any organization today has to deal with radically different forces to its predecessors from generations before. We face massive competition from a new set of global competitors; market and organizational disruption from the relentless advance in technology; seismic shifts in the role of institutions in society; and the changing attitudes of a changing workforce. Oh, and the unstoppable movement towards greater consciousness about what our actions are doing in the world around us – a search for higher meaning and more sustainable behaviours.

So the way in which we distribute power and make decisions simply must evolve. Contemporary businesses that intuitively get this are creating genuinely innovative methods for decision making, and also reviving ancient models that have been pooh-poohed in business circles.

At their very core, these organizations are flipping convention on its head and showing us all smarter, more profitable and way cooler ways to get decisions made at work.

The very idea of 'democracy' (did you just say DEMOCRACY?) at work is seen as subversive, 'participation' is seen as a nice to have, whilst collaboration is increasingly an empty buzzword, thanks to technology vendors banging on endlessly about how their system will enhance collaboration.

I first came across the idea of democracy at work while sat at my desk in my first (and only) job after dropping out of university. I was enjoying my work and my progress, and had clambered out of telemarketing (the horror) into product marketing where, in this medium-sized telecommunications company, the fun happened. I loved my peers, I respected my boss, and the work was fun. The problems was that I'd just had a terrible annual review in which I requested that my pay was raised to the same level as a much older, but not terribly high-performing, colleague. My boss replied: 'you're doing well for your age'. What?! At that point I felt I had to get myself into an environment where my age would not limit my progress, and I was fortunate to stumble upon the websites of the American entrepreneurial magazines, *Inc.* and *Fast Company*. I began to get excited about the dream of starting my own thing. And browsing Inc.com one day I found an article that changed my life.

Called 'The Power of Listening' and written in 2003, the article tells the story of a corrugated box factory business owned by two Harvard-educated graduates, the Centenari brothers (there's a link to the full article in 'Further Reading' at the end of this chapter). In this commoditized, tough market, the brothers initially followed conventional business management practices. After all, they'd both been through Harvard Business School. However, after surviving a tough period, they started to see the light and – as the business prospered – came across ideas about open book management and other enlightened practices. They soon found themselves reading *Maverick* by Ricardo Semler, in which the author, a Brazilian CEO, created an absolutely bonkers approach to business which saw his own manufacturing company thrive. (And, by the way, *Maverick* is a popular book and has been around for a while – people you may not expect to actually have read it may well have done, including potential new hires; it can be a bit like the secret handshake of this progress business movement, 'oh, you've read *Maverick*' with a nod and knowing smile!)

The Centenaris, now inspired, went on to implement all kinds of radical practices, including open book accounting and voting on key decisions (sometimes resulting in decisions going in the opposite direction to what the brothers hoped for). I printed this article off and vowed that one day this would be how my business would operate.

A year or so later, I gave that printed article to my new business partner Tom Nixon and it blew his mind too. We both then devoured *Maverick* by Ricardo Semler which became our bible, and the seeds of our own company were sown.

But why? What was it that compelled all of these people to do things differently? Why would we, you or, indeed, anyone want to run businesses democratically?

WHY MAKE DECISIONS AND DISTRIBUTE POWER DIFFERENTLY?

So why do these new, more social businesses establish alternative, and seemingly subversive, democratic approaches to decision making? This is hippy stuff, right? 'So you all sit around in a big circle *every time* you want to make a decision?' Cue roll of eyes. Love it!

The simple answer is: because it makes sense. Business-sense. Society-sense. People-sense.

And in five or ten years' time, this is going to be mainstream. (It is already becoming so, and rapidly). And, by then, the window of opportunity and advantage for the courageous and the 'irrational' – that's you, I hope – will have passed. Now is the time!

Here are some of the major factors driving our organizations to make decision making happen in more democratic ways:

1 Linus' Law
2 Gen Y

3 Realtime

4 The internet

1 LINUS' LAW

Linus Torvalds is the initiator of the Linux operating system, which runs on the ten fastest supercomputers in the world and is the basis for Google's Android. Linus' Law is named after him. The Law states that 'with enough eyeballs, all bugs are shallow'. A bug is a problem or glitch that a lone developer gets stuck on and cannot fix. By opening up that problem to a broader base of participation, as Torvalds did through developing the rock-solid technology Linux, all bugs become 'shallow'.

The Open Source model – underpinned by the wisdom of Linus' Law – has proven to be enormously successful and we all benefit from it. We live in a world where great chunks of the internet are run on Open Source software, powering the internet servers through which your information flows every day. Software like Apache server, which runs 65% of internet servers, and the Mozilla Firefox browser, are created and developed by small and large communities of software developers that have often never physically met.

Vitally, Linux and Open Source software in general are seen by the developer community to be more secure, more robust and more reliable than the proprietary alternatives: because the sunlight of transparency shines into their code, because of Linus' Law.

Working together in a flat, loosely connected network, in a peer-to-peer fashion, is behind the most significant advance in human society in the last thousand years (that's the internet). What Linus' Law tells us is how an inclusive approach to management and production can lead to much higher-quality end results. This is one of the factors driving organizations towards more democratic approaches to decision making.

So, the question for us in today's organizations is, are we getting enough of the right eyeballs on this problem and, if not, how can we solve it through a different approach to the decisions we make about our work? Have the democratic contributions of many helped to create the best possible solution?

2 MANAGING GEN Y

A second driver for more democratic, participative approaches at work is that your team and your wider organization is filling up with Gen Y, who are increasingly becoming a significant part of the workforce. These guys just will not accept top-down. Having grown up in a different world, they have radically different expectations from work. 'In the workplace, Gen Y tends to favour an inclusive style of management, dislike slowness, and desire immediate feedback about performance (Francis-Smith, 2004). And again: 'Speed, customization, and interactivity – two-way nonpassive engagement – are likely to help keep Gen Y focused' (Martin and Tulgan, 2004). You will fail if you do not involve these guys. But get them on board, include and engage them in the decisions that affect them, and you'll fly!

There are two big benefits here. First, by actively involving your teams in the making of decisions, you will improve the quality of those decisions (Linus' Law). Second, working with your people and, in particular, those from Gen Y you will be significantly enhancing their engagement with those better quality decisions, their willingness to follow through and their hearts and minds.

So, Gen Y's arrival provides us with a huge opportunity to evolve the way in which decision making happens.

3 REALTIME

A third and compelling driver for more approaches that empower our whole organization is that this massively connected and rapidly evolving world is moving at a pace that our organizations are struggling to keep up with. There's a whole chapter on this later on in the book (see Chapter Six – Change Velocity). But, in brief, these days we simply cannot wait for messages to filter up and then back down when the events and information flowing around our markets move so quickly. A PR guy from a major European rail operator said at an event we were both contributing to: 'when there was a crisis we used to have twenty minutes before the news broke during which time we could get a handle on the situation; today we have twenty seconds.' Gulp.

Funnily enough, the objection to participative and empowered forms of decision-making is often that 'we don't have the time!' Perhaps the real challenge is that we do not have the time to go through the conventional decision-making processes, to reach bottlenecks, to wait for a pending decision to ping around the organization whilst change and disruption happens in the real world. Perhaps it is a bit like the aphorism 'I couldn't afford to buy cheap' – counter-intuitive, speaking to the pressures that are faced, but cutting through the crap.

So with the realtime nature of the world we now operate and live in, we need to reshape and upgrade the decision making infrastructure to keep us moving at the same speed as the world outside our four walls.

4 THE INTERNET

The fourth factor driving change in decision-making proc-esses is (drumroll!) the internet! In their prophetic, brilliant work the authors of *The Cluetrain Work* wrote, back in 1999, that 'Hyperlinks subvert hierarchy'. As they foresaw, in a world where the internet massively connects at all levels, regardless of title and office in the formal hierarchies, our influence and attention flows to the person that can actually fix the problem.

For example, in my first and only proper job, there was a lovely receptionist called Margaret. A long-standing loyal employee, Margaret had little formal power or influence. But once you got to know the business, you knew that there were a whole load of questions and issues to which only Margaret would know the answer.

Today, the Margarets of this world are connected to many more people that seek answers: and so we see the rise of the engineer who voluntarily fixes customer problems out of hours on Twitter; the senior manager who listens and joins in anonymously with real customers to understand their genuine and unfiltered feedback in forums that she just cannot access through conventional means; and the growth of new teams and roles to provide customer service in the social web in response to sub-set of customers who know that they can get the fastest response to their issue by kicking up a fuss in the public social web. Hyperlinks have indeed subverted hierarchy. Your organizational structure either helps that, or gets in the way. And, as a result, the manner in which our people are empowered has a direct knock-on effect on the way our organization performs.

THE PRIZE OF PARTICIPATIVE WORKING

Given these four factors, contemporary organizations are employing the power of democracy to create smarter approaches to decision making. That leads to very powerful and tangible business benefits, including:

- Highest levels of engagement from their workforce, which is consistently proven to drive profitability.
- Attract the very best talent, including from Gen Y (more on this in Chapter Three: Progressive People).
- Increased collaboration, leading to greater innovation and less over-dependence on a few 'knowledge hoarders'.

- Improved ability to adapt internally more quickly in an unpredictable and highly adaptive environment.
- Improved ability to communicate effectively at the new speed of business, which is closer and closer to realtime thanks to technology (see Chapter Seven: Tech DNA).

SO WHAT DOES DEMOCRACY IN BUSINESS LOOK LIKE?

To make this practical and helpful we need to break this down into three sections:

- Ethos and principles
- Decision-making approaches
- Underlying motivations

ETHOS AND PRINCIPLES

First, to really make this work you have to believe in some basic principles. And the fundamental principle is this: 'I believe that we can get better results by involving more of the right people'.

If you cannot believe that, you will get stuck here. It really is that simple. You have to believe and to see that opening issues and decisions up to more of the right people will lead to a better end result. Like anything new, it is a leap of faith. And once you've leapt, you'll get the rewards. But to take that first leap you must believe that it can be better.

Second, you must put your power into the process and then be willing to live with the consequences. Until you

have sat with a decision that is close to being made, that is
no longer in your hands, and that is tantalizingly close to
being the very opposite outcome to that you had hoped for,
you have not truly empowered and fuelled this approach to
decision making. It must be real, and every individual must
throw themselves into making it real. If there is any hint
that either you may not fully back the decision that is made
by the group or that you are only chucking soft, easy unimportant issues into group decision-making processes then
you will fail. It's gotta be real! That's where the huge potential lies – in the reality and the excitement and the shared
power of carving out real decisions together.

These two requirements are, by far, the hardest because
they are the highest order. Everything else is just detail.
Easy, right?

However, for those who feel scared off by suddenly
handing over the keys to their unruly internal mob there
are intermediary steps that can be taken on the journey.

In my own company's experience we have graduated
from making relatively unimportant decisions together like
'shall we shut down the office between Christmas and the
New Year?', through to much more impactful and meaningful decisions, such as, 'shall we reject this potential new
client on ethical grounds?' and 'what should the CEO's
rewards package be this year?'

There is no right or wrong way to go about this. No
approved approach. As we go further, you will find ways to
take the organization you are involved with on their own
journey.

Decision-making approaches

There are a number of decision-making approaches that are well evolved and described elsewhere including:

- Democractic
- Sociocratic/consensus
- Empowered individuals or groups

We will look at how to begin implementing these in more detail after looking at some of the companies leading the way in this area.

Underlying motivations

When you're operating in an environment where the idea of participation in decision making is the very last thing on anyone's mind, it can be hard to connect with the idea that other people in the organization might be motivated to get involved in more decision making. From that cynical mindset, it can sound or feel a bit like this: 'why on earth would our employee want to do that – surely they just want to come in to work, go home and have an easy life?' For some people that may be true, but wouldn't you say that most people have ideas and contributions to make that go beyond a 'head down' 9 to 5 existence?

We have trouble in the business community remembering that there are broader motivations beyond money alone.

In Chapter Three: Progressive People, this is something we look at in more detail and, in particular, the work of Professor Steven Reiss and his 16 basic desires theory. Looking at this list, I believe that at least seven of those basic desires can be powerful motivators to get involved in participative decision making:

- Idealism, the need for social justice
- Independence, the need for individuality
- Order, the need for organized, stable, predictable environments
- Power, the need for influence of will
- Status, the need for social standing/importance
- Tranquility, the need to be safe
- Vengeance, the need to strike back/to win

All of these are stores of latent energy just waiting to be tapped through democractic decision-making approaches. Just imagine:

'This is my chance to try to make this unfair company policy so much fairer'. 'This is our opportunity to exert some control over what goes on around here'.

Wouldn't it be good to tap into deep motivations like these in yourself and the people around you?

WHO CAN WE BE INSPIRED BY?

To make more sense of these ideas and theories, let's take a look at some organizations that are already reaping the rewards.

NAMASTÉ SOLAR

Namasté Solar is a rapidly growing solar power business based in Boulder, Colorado. Providing solar energy tech-

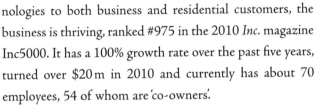

nologies to both business and residential customers, the business is thriving, ranked #975 in the 2010 *Inc.* magazine Inc5000. It has a 100% growth rate over the past five years, turned over $20 m in 2010 and currently has about 70 employees, 54 of whom are 'co-owners'.

Their extraordinary growth figures aren't all that's exciting about the company. For starters, Namasté started as a pure, out-and-out co-operative, hence the 'co-owners'. Over time, Namasté has responded to its own evolution and the changes in the world around it, and continues to adapt the way it operates to this present day. These structures do not need to be rigid and inflexible, which is a theme we return to in Chapter Eight: Fair Finances.

Hearing Blake Jones from Namasté Solar talk about the business, the structure and, in particular, how decision making is managed, is refreshingly clear. The Namasté approach has five levels at which decisions are made:

1 Individual level: 'On the individual level, the company is a "meritocracy" whereby individuals can assume responsibilities based on proven competencies and feel empowered to make decisions.'
2 Peer review level: 'Peer review refers to a process whereby an individual co-owner consults with multiple other co-owners to resolve the issue.'
3 Committee level: 'When more in-depth discussion and collaboration is required, the issue is addressed by one of the company's many "committees," which consist of volunteers; and "teams," which consist of members grouped together based upon job role.'

4 Company level: 'A company-wide vote is required when a new or particularly important issue is introduced. The issue is then addressed by the entire company via a democratic voting process.'

5 Board level: 'In the rare event that a resolution is not made at the first four levels of decision making, the board of directors, which consists of five elected co-owners (any co-owner may nominate themselves for board elections), is empowered to intervene and provide resolution.'

Can you see how this pushes decision-making power into the hands of Namasté's team of 70 or so people?

Rather than a default of either individual managers or the exec team, the whole company is empowered and people are encouraged to resolve issues at the early stage levels wherever possible.

What is also striking about the Namasté model is the breadth of available options in how to get a decision made, without it being overwhelming or cluttered. There is no default decision-making location, nor a sense of a particular bottleneck slowing the organization down.

What would it be like to work in an organization where the decision making was so clearly expressed and so evenly distributed?

By the way, all of this does not mean to say that the board luxuriate in an easy-going world where no tough decisions ever get to them. The board is often called upon to make important and challenging decisions, which is why it's so important to Namasté that each of the board members is held accountable to the co-owners. In addition to having relatively short, two-year terms, all board members must be democratically elected by co-owners on a one-person, one-vote basis. Seriously cool company.

Namasté in 2010: $20 m revenues; 70 employees (of which, 54 co-owners).

HCL TECHNOLOGIES

HCL Technologies is a leading global IT services company that focuses on 'transformational outsourcing'. Headquartered in Noida, India, the company has over 80,000 employees located in offices in 26 countries and works with a customer base across many industries including financial services, manufacturing, consumer services, public services and healthcare. The business has a turnover in the order of $4 bn a year. Not small beer!

Like many people, I hadn't heard the story of HCL Technologies (HCLT) until I came across the book *Employees First, Customers Second* by CEO, Vineet Nayar. It's a great tale of how a big business goes through a transformation – to continue to thrive on a grand scale – through radical new management practices and an ethos that flips the traditional 'customers first' mindset to a position of 'if we do the right thing by our people, our customers will thrive as a result'.

What the HCLT story has done is eliminate, in one fell swoop, the suggestion that participation cannot work, at scale, in business. It also provides a helpful and grounded perspective of what it is like to take a large existing business on such a journey. Case studies like this are few and far between and the early pioneers deserve kudos and support. (Another example worth looking up is the American healthcare company DaVita.)

In *Employees First, Customers Second*, Nayar outlines five brilliant and practical practices that his substantial business put in place:

1 360-degree Survey
2 U&I Portal
3 MyBlueprint
4 Smart Service Desk
5 Employee First Councils

Below, we will look at the first three of these, and I wholeheartedly recommend buying the book to read the whole HCLT story.

1 360-DEGREE SURVEY

As you know, in the classical 360-degree survey an individual gets feedback from all of those around them: from any direct reports if they are a manager, from peers and from their manager and other senior folk. In their 360-degree survey, HCLT went much further than the traditional approach in two ways: first, anyone who felt that a given manager affected their performance could participate in their 360-degree review; second, anyone participating in the survey could then see the results. You can imagine how this creates massively more transparency around reviews and, fundamentally, shifts the responsibility to the managers rather than the employees. In fact, it's a great example of the application of Linus' Law by welcoming in outliers and diverse opinions to create the best possible quality feedback and learning for management. What does this have to do with democracy and empowerment? Everything! This approach massively flattens out hierarchy and reintroduces merit; it shifts power to the grassroots and broadens it out to a wider base and, in doing so, directly influences the power and decision making in HCLT.

Is there a way you can start sharing the results of your own performance review with your team, and invite more people in to review your own performance? We look again at this practice in Chapter Four: Conscious Leadership.

2   U&I PORTAL

Nayar and his team at HCLT designed the U&I platform to effectively open up the CEO's office (and power base) to allow anyone, anywhere in the workforce to ask a question. The platform is available for all in HCLT to see, and the question, the questioner and the answer are all visible.

This profoundly shifts the ability of senior management to hide from difficult questions and promotes the ability of anyone in the organization to ask one.

As Nayar writes, a group of employees told him 'this is the biggest change we have seen at HCLT in years'. This powerful culture change comes from walking the talk, and genuinely opening up the floor to the issues that people in the organization care about. (Similarly, Zappos, a company we look at in the next chapter, has a monthly internal newsletter called 'Ask Anything' where employees can – ahem – ask anything and have their questions answered publicly.)

Is there a way you can use simple, lightweight technology (in small teams, open Q&A or email will suffice!) to get the dirt out and get the 'elephants in the room' talked about and, in doing so, invite more engaged participation from your people?

3 MyBlueprint

Whereas the first two of these management practices are inherently about becoming more participative – through enabling authentic communication and transparency – the third is more fundamental: it is about setting strategy together rather than hierarchically or in silos.

In the MyBlueprint endeavour, HCLT got 300 managers, responsible for business planning in their respective areas, to produce their individual 'blueprints' for the coming year and then share them, together with an audio walkthrough, on a Facebook-like platform called MyBlueprint. These plans were then made available to a further 8000 managers to consume, review and give feedback.

The results speak for themselves: 'Everyone felt able to contribute to the thinking and planning process. People understood the challenges better, owned the plan, and could align themselves with the strategy as I had never seen before.'

This is the power of deep, meaningful participation in the running of our organizations – to get better solutions, more belief and higher levels of engagement. HCL is an inspiring and instructional example of how very large businesses can do just that.

> HCL Technologies in 2011: $3 bn revenues; 82,000 employees.

APPLE AND VISIONARY LEADERS – THE ANTI-EXAMPLES?

One of the great unresolved tensions for me in the democratic model is best summarized by the question: 'what about Apple then?' According to the mythology and the literature, Apple was run by Steve Jobs in a tightly controlled and extremely hierarchical way. Whole departments were locked down in secrecy, people worked on tiny segments of the visionary product in development – never seeing the whole of what they were contributing to until the very end. Jobs was himself apparently incredibly harsh in his dealings with people.

If all of this is true, then it really does sound as if Apple is a powerful anti-example of the democratic mode of working, truly the antithesis of Linus' Law: here, rather than many eyeballs, there were just a few of the 'right' eyeballs.

And, in that model, the company created some of the greatest product designs of the late twentieth and early twenty-first centuries. It changed the face of the personal computing, music, mobile phone, and (possibly, they gossip at the time of writing) TV industries.

What can be said about this? I do not have the answers, at least not yet. Perhaps there is something about the resilience of a business so dependent on a few visionaries. It sounds churlish to say it after Jobs' death, but it is true that the company was not just dependent on him but on a number of key people. Perhaps, also, there is then something about an organization's life span when it is so dependent on a visionary individual. Maybe the democratic model can provide a platform for a longer period than the led-by-a-few model?

And, beyond Apple, and back into the community of democratically run businesses, there is the common thread of visionary leadership. It seems to be both a paradox and a simple fact of life that to involve the many needs the vision and energy of just one or two: Semler at Semco (mentioned in the introduction to this chapter), Blake at Namasté, Vineet at HCL, and still more – the visionary CEO Kent who turned around DaVita (briefly referenced but not looked at in this book). Or perhaps the world lionizes the few leaders progressive enough to see these opportunities and committed enough to see them through – perhaps that's it. They are over-celebrated simply because they are so different.

I do not know the answers, but if we are to grow this movement and if you are to carry your own changes through then we must at least glimpse into the dark spots and challenge what we find.

How can you begin the journey towards democratic working?

By now you're probably ready for something concrete, if not desperate to get away from the polemic and on to practical steps!

Here's how to make it happen:

1 Acknowledge that it is a journey
2 Communicate the dream and the benefits
3 Share the load
4 Ready, Fire, Aim

1 ACKNOWLEDGE THAT IT IS A JOURNEY

It is a journey for Namasté and HCL and it is an ongoing journey for political democracies around the world and has been for millennia.

Making democracy work is an iterative process. So you're not going to get this done in one step, nor are your supporters, your partners or your colleagues. Acknowledge that. Recognize also that this will require huge patience. It will take time. It will be hard work and there absolutely will be challenges.

A case in point: in our company our most recent decision-making challenge concerned paternity pay, brought up by two expectant fathers, both brilliant and loyal team members. For some reason, the way we'd previously made such decisions just didn't work for this issue – the team size had grown, we'd had a slow summer which meant we were all cautious about finances, previous 'benefits' requests and suggestions had been voted out in a collective budgeting process. The context had changed, but our patched-together and learnt-on-the-job methods had not.

In the first round discussion, which was intended to be lightweight, the potential decision was not clearly defined, the options or outcomes un-investigated, the method for making the decision together unclear and unpracticed. It got ugly, quickly.

In the second round we tried again, but still it was hard, demoralizing and began to test important relationships between colleagues and peers. I felt under huge pressure to deliver a positive result (or at least a conclusion of some kind!) and pressure to keep the group together and relationships intact. The proposers felt isolated, anxious and increasingly bitter. The wider team felt encumbered, distracted and irritated. This was hardly decision making at realtime speed!

In the end, we called in some friends we'd met through WorldBlu community – the leadership and culture development consultancy Future Considerations. Their support was utterly invaluable. Mark Young, their CEO, facilitated the discussions and taught us a new framework for making group decisions and helped us make key choices about how future decisions would be made.

We have more work to do: tidying up what was agreed in this last round of decision making, getting it documented, reinforcing the new methods to the whole team. It is a journey.

Manage your own expectations. Remind yourself of the goals, the vision, the benefits. Keep the faith when times are tough!

2 COMMUNICATE THE DREAM AND THE BENEFITS

Without the belief of those around you, the whole effort to engender democracy at work is utterly meaningless. What you are doing is taking the alternative path, you are taking the pioneering left-turn when the world will expect you to take the tried-and-tested right turn.

To begin with there are two elements to winning support: the Dream and the Benefits.

The Dream is the vision, the higher ground that you're aiming for, the golden-sunshine-infused meadow where life is good and the butterflies flit happily from flower to flower. Life is good here! This is the emotional half of the message, appealing to the right side of the brain and the heart.

The Benefits are the benefits! The positive outcomes that will flow from democracy at work. To find these, you need to locate concrete, tangible answers to the question 'what's in this for me/us?' They need to be business-oriented, measurable and designed to appeal to the most sceptical, reluctant people in your organization. This is the factual half of the message, appealing to the left side of the brain.

You can find some high-level benefits a bit earlier in this chapter.

Later, you have a much more powerful lever than the Dream and the Benefits – which is the energy and commitment generated by people proposing and then seeing through decisions, from participating in major decisions and having their say. That's the super-powerful-magic-fairy-dust – a truly unstoppable and un-fakeable force. At this point the whole idea of democracy at work becomes a powerful reality and not just a pipedream, but first you have to get them to this point.

3 SHARE THE LOAD

You cannot do this alone. Nor should you (it's democracy!). Seek out those who you know intuitively find this exciting and create a core. Encourage each member of the group to buy their own copy of *Maverick* by Ricardo Semler (or maybe *Employees First, Customers Second* if you're in a very large corporation), and then come together to swap notes.

If it fits with your organizational culture, give the group a name – whether it's a working group or a council is up to you (but for now, I'd recommend staying away from the word 'committee' as it will only excite the sceptics). Invite this group to be the project team, the people that are going to make it happen. Create the plan together, meet regularly and do stuff in between – and as you do, you spread the expertise, the belief and create a vital resilience to the whole endeavour.

This group's key responsibilities should be to create, over time, a decision-making framework that is as clear and comprehensive as Namasté Solar's and to provide the organizational learning necessary to practically produce good quality decisions through such a framework – that is, by providing the opportunities to practice and learn.

In sharing the load, be sure also to get connected with other people who are taking this alternative path. One of the things that happens when you start to take this alternative approach to business is that your peer group drops from squillions of everyday, conventional businesses to a much smaller, tighter set of organizations. And, as a result, it can be hard not to feel alone.

One group we found really helpful is a feisty, networked organization called WorldBlu which is without peer in the job that it does connecting up progressive leaders and entrepreneurs. Through the annual WorldBlu List of Most Democratic Companies, the organization builds pride and profile for the community, but vitally that list is based on a comprehensive surveying tool which is extremely useful in benchmarking where your organization is on the journey to becoming as democratic as it can be.

Traci Fenton founded WorldBlu with a mission to spread the concept of democracy at work. This dedicated group of people works tirelessly towards its mission of seeing one billion people employed in democratic organizations. Gob-smackingly cool. Talk about a Purpose of Significance.

Call WorldBlu and see if they can help you connect with other organizations locally to you with similar values who are on their own journey. Get them to share their experiences with your group or your whole organization.

Finally, encourage scepticism and challenge within your internal group – if you are to carry this thing through you will need to be familiar and comfortable with the downsides. The group must be pragmatic optimists, not whimsical evangelists.

4 READY, FIRE, AIM

At some point you have to just start. JFDI, as some people say. Or Ready, Fire, Aim. Because this is a journey and inherently a learning experience, it has to be iterative. Given that it is iterative, the sooner you start, the sooner you and your organization begin to benefit from the learning. Waiting merely postpones that learning.

Once this is no longer just a personal crusade and you have some kind of group belief emerging, find a decision to make in a democratic way.

Set expectations for what might happen during this first and inevitably slightly haphazard session, remind yourselves of the Dream and the Vision, have a go at making a decision together, and then find an appropriate way to celebrate. A first experience of making a democratic decision at work is a massive milestone that most people have not achieved in their careers. Well done!

SPECIFIC PROCESSES AND TOOLS

In practical terms, when we consider how to make such decisions, it's useful to look at some of the most frequently used approaches.

ONE PERSON ONE VOTE

The simplest manifestation of democracy is 'one person equals one vote'. In this mode, you will need to agree what your quorum is – that is, the minimum necessary number of people to make a decision collectively – and agree what percentage of votes can carry a decision. These are important design decisions and they can be moulded over time. To begin with, go with something simple like 80% of the whole team/organization makes quorum and 'most votes wins'.

'One person one vote' is an attractive place to start because it is so damn simple. Hard to go wrong. However, in time, some people find its simplicity frustrating – this approach can create winners and losers in each decision, and sometimes the losing group can be just less than 50% of the whole team or company – which could be quite demotivating to a big and important chunk of people. This is why sociocracy and ideas of consensus have emerged, and these are described in just a sec.

WORLDBLU SCORECARD

To support its mission to see one billion people working in democratically run organizations, WorldBlu has developed a scorecard, which is delivered through an online survey platform. As you might expect, the scorecard is fantastic in helping you to benchmark where your organization is today against a set of particular criteria that the WorldBlu team have developed, and against a deep body of data accumulated over years of use with other organizations across different industries, sizes and geographies.

To use the scorecard you will need to become WorldBlu members, which brings a number of invaluable benefits, not least because using this resource alone is very highly recommended.

CONSENSUS AND SOCIOCRACY

Some organizations practising democracy at work find themselves putting into practice more 'evolved' decision-making practices that introduce some subtlety and simple sophistication into proceedings. Sociocracy is an approach that many turn to.

A quick caveat: in my opinion the implementation of sociocracy is hugely powerful and we are at the early stages of implementing it at my workplace, however it *is* a discipline or system in its own right which requires some in-depth learning and practising. So here in Culture Shock we're going to take a look at the principles, but you will need to find out more (unless you are some kind of decision-making genius) before implementing these ideas at work. Health warning over!

Having been coined some 70 or so years earlier in the late 19th century by a French philosopher, sociocracy in its current form was developed in the mid-20th century by two enlightened Dutch guys – first an educator called Kees Boeke, and then later his student Gerard Endenburg.

The essence of sociocracy is this: that in democracy, where one person has one vote, the minority yield to the majority, and often that minority is made up of a large group of people who often are left with a decision which is a long way from meeting their needs. So, rather than reaching a compromise, the group – be that a voting population or a 20-person company – is riven down the centre between two or more distinct camps. Sociocracy instead aims to create decisions which are created collaboratively by the group, and which – in the end – are satisfactory to the entire group. This means that at the point of a decision being agreed, no one in the group has a remaining objection. Sounds dreamy eh?

SO HOW ON EARTH DOES IT WORK?

Endenburg, who took the earlier work on sociocratic decision making and applied it when he took over his parents' electrical engineering business, outlined four design principles or 'rules':

1 Decision making on policy issues by consent
2 Organizing in circles
3 Double-linking
4 Elections by consent

1 DECISION MAKING ON POLICY ISSUES BY CONSENT

While operational decisions can be made using whichever form of decision-making the group agrees on (for example, using one person, one vote, or empowering a CEO or a committee to make decisions in a given area), all policy issues are decided upon using consent. (Consent means no one has a concern with the potential that is so big that they 'can't live with it'. In consenting, everyone can live with the decision proposed, even if it is a long way from their ideal.)

2 ORGANIZING IN CIRCLES

One of the most interesting aspects for me is how sociocracy uses circles to organize. So a consultancy like ours might have a leadership circle, an innovation circle, a clients' circle and a marketing circle. Each circle has responsibility for a given area that has been formally delegated to it, and is semiautonomous (almost like terrorist cells – sorry if that's a big or uncomfortable leap!). In normal business language, a circle might look after responsibilities just as a working group, a committee, programme team or steering group – but circles behave very differently due to their decision-making approach within the group.

3 DOUBLE-LINKING

The concept of the double-link is what joins up the sociocratic organization from being an otherwise disconnected jumble of autonomous circles – it's a beautiful piece of design thinking. Circles are actually hierarchical: each circle sends a representative to the circle above them and the circle above them sends a representative back too. So, in every circle, there are two members who also take full part in a higher and lower circle, apart from at the highest circle – usually like a board of directors or executive team, which has a representative from the next circle down, but cannot send anyone any higher! This structure of circles is what binds the sociocratic organization together, each double-link providing conduits, carrying information and creating vital connectivity.

4 ELECTIONS BY CONSENT

Roles and responsibilities within circles, including being a representative on another circle, are agreed upon within the group through consent. So you can see how flat and participative these structures are. It's like this: 'OK, we're the marketing circle, these are our goals as determined by the rest of the organization, so what are the roles we need to divide up – who's going to do what?' That is the semi-autonomous power that a circle has.

If this interests you, definitely find out more. There is a community of believers and practitioners out there, and role model organizations that are performing well using these practices, plus a metric boatload of online resources and books.

On the topic of consent in decision making, I was lucky enough to hear Larry Dressler, a true master of collaborative decision making, share his stories and experiences at the WorldBlu Live conference. Larry has written two books, *Consensus Through Conversation* and *Standing In The Fire*. These are mentioned in the Further Reading section below.

THE DARK SIDE OF DEMOCRACY AT WORK

Before finishing this chapter it is very important to acknowledge that – in addition to the questions highlighted earlier about the tension between visionary leaders and broad participation – democracy at work is not always the easiest policy to take or to stick with.

Democratic decision making can feel slow and costly: sometimes it requires the involvement of many rather than just a few; sometimes decisions can require lots of people to invest quite a bit of time (a thorough conversation can take several hours). In a context of urgent business pressures and the need to get things done, that can be very hard to stomach – especially for those who remain on the fence.

The questions here are:

- What does it cost us to make a poorer-quality decision – one that has not been tested by a diverse set of personalities and experiences?
- What does it cost us to make a decision that no one believes in or will commit to, or will even actively resist?
- Are our decision-making processes pushing enough responsibility down to the individual or 'in small groups' level, or are we trying to do too much with everyone involved?

In a well-designed, democratically run organization, decisions are absolutely quicker because they are made at or very close to the point where they need to be made – in the thick of it.

Even so, in certain circumstances it cannot be doubted that, at times, democratic decision making is slower and costlier in the early stages, though the implementation may be much faster and smoother. To make real change we must acknowledge this and communicate it.

SUMMARY

In the first chapter we looked at purpose – the fundamental of *why* your organization exists. This chapter has been much more about *how* your organization behaves – looking at how the brain, how the operating system makes decisions.

As more businesses around the world shift these two building blocks – their fundamental 'why' and their 'how' – so does the whole fabric of business change bit by bit. I think that is pretty cool.

Indeed, if we as a community of progressive business people do only two things, it is these two that will drive the biggest changes. By doing so, we will participate in organizations creating results full of meaning, operating with methods full of engagement.

If you wish, you can stop reading now. I do not jest. There is more. But everything that follows is built on these two cornerstones. So if you can work on just two things, work on these.

Unlock the potential of your people, and let them work towards a Purpose of Significance. That is a change worth seeing in the world.

FURTHER READING

- 'The Power of Listening': http://bit.ly/cltrshk4
- *Maverick* and *The Seven Day Weekend* by Ricardo Semler, WorldBlu
- *Employees First, Customers Second* by Vineet Nayar, HCL
- *Freedom at Work* by Traci Fenton, WorldBlu
- *Consensus Through Conversation* and *Standing In The Fire.* by Larry Dressler

CHAPTER THREE

PROGRESSIVE PEOPLE

Having now looked at Purpose and Meaning, and Democracy and Empowerment, let us now consider the topic of Progressive People in detail.

In theory, people should be the great beneficiaries of business. After all, we're people – we work in businesses, we own businesses, we created businesses and, for the most part, accept and depend on businesses.

So shouldn't then people love business, and thrive in and because of business? Instead business seems to be the enemy of people. It – this horrible machine we created – spits people out embittered, exhausted, demoralized on a daily basis and over years and careers.

We have all allowed for people and humanity and authenticity and real lives to be different to professionalism and work and business. We have allowed these two halves of the same sphere to be kept apart rather than held together. It became acceptable to only look for enjoyment in the evenings and weekends – work was just *work*.

Given this backdrop, we all know innately and absolutely that business must radically change how it treats people. We have all seen people around us be dreadfully mistreated by businesses and business people. We have all seen documentaries or read articles about the exploitation that happens to poorer people around the world at the hands of business to satisfy our own consumer needs and wants.

This. Must. Stop. The thing is, it really doesn't need to be this way.

BEING BAD TO PEOPLE IS BEING BAD TO THE BOTTOM LINE

Aside from the moral imperative to treat people better in business there are profound and proven business benefits going untapped. It is well understood by the human resources community that engagement translates into profit. It is well understood by managers that a great, motivated team member is worth five or ten or even twenty poor, switched-off team members. Yet we seem to do everything we can in conventional business to destroy engagement and to run roughshod over the simple opportunities to create a better environment for people.

What a terrible shame! And yet what a huge opportunity. For people are the lifeblood of any business, and in the 21st century we are already seeing the pioneering social businesses celebrating and unlocking the abilities of their people and the people around them in ways that create powerful value.

WHAT DOES THE PROGRESSIVE BUSINESS MOVEMENT DO DIFFERENTLY?

The revolutionaries in this progressive, 21st-century business movement understand this opportunity instinctively and have subverted the ridiculous and staid logic of the last century to create powerful new ways of unleashing and empowering their workforces to create huge value.

Fundamentally, what the smartest organizations do is design for themselves an environment where people can thrive and achieve more, and feel stronger than they ever believed they could about their working lives.

These organizations place the highest premium on people. Not at a lip-service level, but at a deeply ingrained, cultural level.

The newly created value that flows from this approach can be measured financially: better engagement of people translates into profits, sales, lower cost of returns, greater customer lifetime value and so on. But 21st-century social businesses also create value for their people way beyond money alone. As the economist Simon Kuznets, who originally developed the measurement of Gross National Product, said back in 1934: 'the welfare of a nation can scarcely be inferred from a measurement of national income'. We can extend that and suggest that 'the welfare of an organization can scarcely be inferred from financial measures alone'. More of that in Chapter Eight: Fair Finances.

WHAT'S THE PRIZE?

By making challenging but hugely rewarding changes to how people are treated, the following benefits are available to the 21st-century social business:

- Better, faster results through higher workforce engagement.
- Competitive advantage by nurturing innovation and creativity.
- Sustaining competitive advantage by attracting and retaining the very best talent in the hyper-competitive global marketplace.
- A lighter soul and greater well-being for all (from the bottom to the top of an organization) from the knowledge that the business is doing the right thing by its people.

WHERE CAN WE MAKE A DIFFERENCE?

To help you unlock more of these benefits in your team and organization, we're going to look at a set of five Progressive People levers that you can positively pull to jolt your organization into the vanguard:

1 Motivation
2 Happiness
3 Rewards
4 Environment
5 Management

1 MOTIVATION

Given that we can often have trouble in the business community remembering that there are broader motivations than money alone perhaps it is useful to think about the possible motivations for an unpaid volunteer – someone who does what they do just because they do without a pay packet and a boss to distract things. Let's imagine a fervent Wikipedian who has helped write several thousand entries in Wikipedia, has contributed hundreds of hours of her time unpaid, has worked almost entirely without management in the conventional sense, to unpick why people contribute to initiatives.

What would we say are her motivators? Perhaps she is motivated:

- To help other people?
- To share what she knows and cares about?
- To express a passion?
- To be part of something bigger?
- To gain kudos and respect from others?
- Because she simply enjoys it!?

Whichever of those it is, you know intuitively that in yourself these motivators are much more powerful than money alone. Consequently, tens of millions of hours of volunteer time has gone into the production of Wikipedia, a marvellous testament to what we can achieve when we work together, while many of us are sat on the sofa watching TV.

And, in writing this list, it occurred to me that it was very likely that someone clever has studied this. Turns out they have!

MOTIVATION: THE 16 BASIC DESIRES THEORY

Having studied some 6000 people, a certain Professor Steven Reiss proposed a theory that found 16 basic desires that guide nearly all human behaviour:

- Acceptance, the need for approval
- Curiosity, the need to learn
- Eating, the need for food
- Family, the need to raise children
- Honour, the need to be loyal to the traditional values of one's clan/ethnic group
- Idealism, the need for social justice
- Independence, the need for individuality
- Order, the need for organized, stable, predictable environments
- Physical activity, the need for exercise
- Power, the need for influence of will
- Romance, the need for sex
- Saving, the need to collect
- Social contact, the need for friends (peer relationships)
- Status, the need for social standing/importance
- Tranquility, the need to be safe
- Vengeance, the need to strike back/to win

With this in mind, what we need to ask ourselves in business is: which basic desires am I calling upon in our people – which powerful underlying motivations can be harnessed to achieve Purpose of Significance so that we can put a dent in the world?

Perhaps it is also worth us pondering on this: which motivators have been poorly tapped in our organization and, more broadly, in business in the past century? Which can we realistically address and call on? How can we help individuals to match their big motivators with the challenges the company faces?

Let's look at an example of your organization moving into a new area, something that feels like it happens increasingly often. You and your people are going to need to learn about a whole new area, create new relationships, and presumably leave behind some knowledge and relationships that were stable and trusted. This kind of change can be risky and stressful. So, which motivators might be at work for your people that you can help them locate in themselves and harness?

Clearly, curiosity can be a big potential motivator in these circumstances – the need to learn – so try helping the group or individuals to get excited about what isn't yet known, what needs to be discovered and uncovered, and the pathfinding that has to happen. I know that excites me! Maybe, for some people in the group, social contact is a powerful motivator – the opportunity to create new peer relationships, creating exciting new contacts with potential partners, suppliers, customers and so on. Perhaps there's also a tranquillity motivator here too – maybe the new area that you're moving into has the promise of greater stability, more sustainable financial rewards, less competition. Whatever they turn out to be (and of course our motivations are dynamic and shift from minute to minute and year to year in all of us), helping to find the hot buttons in yourself and the people around you can unlock a much more potent and more human set of drivers than the traditional business mode of clumsy financial 'carrots' and fear-and-punishment-based 'sticks'.

2 HAPPINESS

One of the most radical changes in how businesses manage people that is coming down the line is that born out of the growing happiness movement. Top tip: if you want to get a smile out of a 20th-century business executive, tell him or her that happiness is more important than profitability.

But this is no laughing matter. As we touched on earlier in this book, whole nation states are suggesting that measures of happiness will succeed measures of financial productivity. We have outgrown the idea that money alone is the metric and the reason.

This rebalancing to take into account happiness and broader well-being is happening across society and will eventually – and perhaps sooner than we expect – reach the shores of business. As it is, we remain in a fairly sad and turgid state of affairs when it comes to happiness at work, with the annual employee engagement survey (or in the more dynamic organization, not once but twice a year! Let me hear you say 'real time'). The HR community tot up the answers behind closed doors and then send back results to senior management, line managers, and sometimes, to the team's themselves.

As Nic Marks puts it in his readable and very well-referenced ebook *The Happiness Manifesto* 'The time is ripe for our measurement system to shift emphasis from measuring economic production to measuring people's well-being'.

This absolutely applies in a contemporary business. Later in this chapter we will look at how other companies pull this lever and how you can too.

3 REWARDS

All of the academic research says that money is a hygiene factor, by which we mean a factor that needs to be in place and be 'good enough' but beyond that it doesn't actually do much more. I guess most, if not all, of us know that it is terribly demotivating not to be earning 'enough', but when the vast majority of people reach an acceptable base level, increases in earnings are exponentially less effective in increasing personal satisfaction. That's what the science says.

With this in mind, a powerful people lever we have in 21st-century business is to reimagine the whole area of rewards – including, but going beyond, financial rewards and traditional benefits alone.

Here the possibilities are endless, but to remind you of some of them, some organizations include non-financial rewards like:

- Flexible working hours
- Sabbaticals

- Innovation time (Google's famous 20%)
- Duvet days
- Free books (the Zappos library)

Or hear how the legendary Fog Creek Software (www.fogcreek.com) describe their offer to prospective super-talented computer programmers:

> 'Software developers at Fog Creek get spacious, sunlit private offices, unlimited computer gear, electronic height-adjustable desks, Aeron chairs, and a plush office featuring marble showers, a library, a salt water aquarium, professional espresso machine, daily gourmet catered lunch, unlimited snacks, video games and movie nights, and the opportunity to work with a great team.'

Holy moly.

So how can you design a new bundle of progressive rewards? Cor! Well it shouldn't be too hard – this is a FUN task. Talk to or, if you're doing this at scale, survey your people, encourage people to dream, to think about what really matters to them, what they value, what the culture and organizational values are, and to think creatively about what attractive, rewarding and motivating benefits the organization could provide. In my experience the challenging bit will be assessing what the organization can afford, and which investments will create the biggest bang for buck – remembering, of course, that what motivates isn't what costs the most. So Fog Creek's professional espresso machine or movie nights might be high impact and low- or no-cost benefits that actually create great rewards.

4 ENVIRONMENT

Something that smaller businesses and creative services businesses have tended to do much better than large and non-creative services businesses is recognize the impact and value of a positive work environment.

Positive examples are places that feel alive, are comfortable, have a look of being lived in, and clearly value and prioritize the people working in them. People in these offices feel comfortable at work. It doesn't have to be colourful beanbags, but you can generally tell when you walk around a place whether it is people-friendly or not, can't you?

But, these working environments aside, the trend has been heading in the opposite direction.

CNN covered some research from the International Facility Management Association which indicates that the amount of physical space we give our people is drastically shrinking: 'In 1994, the average office worker had 90 square feet of office space, down to 75 square feet in 2010'.

Inevitable in today's climate? Perhaps. But does environment matter to business success? Absolutely. There is plenty of research showing that everything from the colour of the walls to the number of likely interruptions massively affects morale, stress, engagement and, as a result, the bottom line. Take, for example, research cited in a *Wall Street Journal* blog that was carried out by Joan Meyers-

Levy from the University of Minnesota: Meyers-Levy looked at the relationship between ceiling height and thinking style and found that 'when people are in a high-ceilinged room, they're significantly better at seeing the connections between seemingly unrelated subjects'.

Our environment directly influences the quality of the work that we can produce and our well-being, so shouldn't we put more effort into thinking about how to optimize it? To do this I encourage you to go and see other companies' workspaces. Think about space, sunlight, temperature, alternative spaces to the desk for working. And, of course, the internet loves this kind of content – there are plenty of blogs and photo galleries of inspiring offices to help get your creative juices flowing. Again, there are plenty of low-cost, high-impact factors that you can improve if you look for them.

5 MANAGEMENT

The role of line management in actually delivering a contemporary approach to people management is crucial. It is in the nitty gritty of recruitment, day-to-day management and coaching and in performance reviews that many of the available benefits of a new approach to people management are either gained or lost.

The case studies we look at shortly provide many practical examples and bring the whole ethos of progressive management to life but, at this stage, we can break out three specific elements to focus on:

1   Recruitment > Management
2   Coaching > Management
3   Feedback > Reviews

1 RECRUITMENT > MANAGEMENT

In the best run, most progressive businesses, more emphasis is put on the recruitment of team members than on
their subsequent management. There is a belief in these
businesses that – in the words of Jim Collins in *Good to
Great* – if you get 'the right people on the bus' everything
else will sort itself out. So there is a big emphasis on
multiple people being involved in hiring, in hiring being
as much about values as about skills and experiences
and in taking the whole processes of hiring patiently
and thoroughly. Great recruitment shifts the role of
ongoing management from 'managing performance' (a
euphemism for dealing with problems) to genuinely managing performance.

2 COACHING > MANAGEMENT

Second, once the right people are on board, the approach
of these pioneering organizations tends to be on coaching
rather than formal management. That is to say, a style of
working together which empowers, an approach which
helps the individual to find their place, their role, their
hidden talents, rather than telling people what to do, or
placing restrictions on them, or creating highly defined
envelopes to work within. In a coaching culture, the logic
in play is something like 'most people want to be great at

what they do, we spent good time finding them, now let's work on unlocking their full potential'.

3 FEEDBACK > REVIEWS

Third, the approach is to prioritize ongoing and very honest feedback over occasional and scheduled formal reviews. That is not to say that the two are mutually exclusive, but that these cultures tend to prefer the feedback to be continuous, to be in the context of everyday work, and to be unusually honest and real. Remember HCLT's practices? And at Namasté Solar one of their main cultural beliefs is in the importance of 'FOH' – Frank Open Honest communication.

Combined, these three elements make for a powerful new formula in people management.

So, which businesses really celebrate and engage their people?

ZAPPOS

Zappos should be a boring business, shouldn't it? To massively oversimplify, Zappos is a website, a warehouse full of shoes, and a bunch of people answering telephone calls and enquiries. Dull. Like the beige colour of an old PC. Yet Zappos may be the most colourful business making waves at the moment – thanks to its unique culture Zappos is not beige but in fact all the colours of the rainbow, it's not a dull old PC of a business but a graffiti-spray-painted dancing unicorn with a beating heart and crazy eyes.

Zappos is essentially built around the principle that if you create the environment, hire the right people and so develop the right culture, you will thrive. And Zappos is delivering against that belief with a thriving business: widely recognized to be the largest online shoe retailer in the US, it was bought by Amazon in 2009 for about $1.2 bn, and is believed to turn over in excess of $1 bn per annum.

For the whole story, you must read CEO Tony Hsieh's book *Delivering Happiness*. But looking at just a few of Zappos practices should help inspire us all.

FAMILY

Zappos staff use the word 'family' a lot. Not just when they speak or write, but publicly on their website and in company materials and their annual *Culture Book*.

The *Culture Book* itself is worth a look – it's a year-book, 'a collage of unedited submissions from employees', that gives every employee the opportunity to say what they feel and think about the company. The *Culture Book* is a sweet and powerful example of how the many people make up the whole organization, and how progressive businesses don't pretend or hide that fact but instead celebrate it.

Back to the 'family' word though: the great thing is if you say you're a family, then you have to live up to it. This is not 'employee relations' – the whole thing is powerfully reframed in a way that leads to an entirely different approach at Zappos.

CREATE FUN AND A LITTLE WEIRDNESS

Zappos has ten Zappos Family Core Values. Core value number 3 is 'Create Fun And A Little Weirdness'. I just love that! And this value clearly permeates everything that Zappos does: from the exuberant All-Hands meetings, to the chaotic office decor, through to the stringent hiring processes. What could be further from the conventional brainwashing about how people should behave at work? We don't want you to be 'professional', we want you to be WEIRD.

REPLY-ALL HAT

One of my favourite Zappos people initiatives is their Reply-All hat. You know that moment when, in a medium or large-sized organization, you or someone you know unwittingly replies to ALL? Ouchy! At Zappos, to celebrate that moment, they have a Reply-All hat. Not just any hat, this is a gaudy, ridiculous plumed showgirl hat, and if you are unlucky enough to have Replied-All, you wear the hat and have to parade around the Zappos offices while being shouted and whistled at. You also are at risk of having photos taken, or even a video made (have a look on YouTube)! It is as brilliant and mad and awful as it sounds, and I for one wish our team was big enough to warrant one!

ZAPPOS TOURS AND *HAPPINESS DELIVERED*

The Zappos culture is so potent that they are increasingly sought out to spread their ideas. They offer free, daily tours (and will even pick you up in a minibus from your Vegas hotel). Their inspiring CEO Tony Hseih has written a book called *Happiness Delivered*, spreading their ideas. They also now have a part of the business called Zappos Insights to provide training and consultancy services to other businesses.

Can you see how engaging the Zappos culture is to people like you and me? And also how straightforward it is – completely unlike traditional business, but completely human and immediately recognizable as fun *and* smart ways to go about things? A great company.

W. L. Gore & Associates

W. L. Gore & Associates is quite a mysterious business. The makers of many innovative textiles including Gore-Tex, the well-known breathable waterproof fabric, the company has an extremely interesting approach to people and structure.

What must be said is that, for Gore, these practices are not new. Though the ranting and railing in this book is against the staid, stupid mainstream management practices of the 20th century, Gore is a 20th-century success – Bill Gore founded the business with his wife Vieve in 1958! Their practices, some formed way back then, are still revolutionary today.

Team size and lattice structure

One of the few things that is reasonably well known in the business community about Gore, which remains to this day a privately-held enterprise, is its unconventional practices around organizational structure. Fifty years ago they must have seemed genuinely bonkers, but today – though still unconventional – can seem much smarter.

Gore's structure is made up of two particularly interesting components: their team size and their lattice structure.

Team-wise, the business operates very small plants – typically a maximum of 250 people in each. So, for every 250 people, the organization has to provide a different building and replicate the same core structure that a single plant requires. We can safely assume that there are inefficiencies here in staff, in building costs, in equipment. Everything is replicated rather than lumped into the same ever-growing mega-plant! But in the words of their current CEO Terri Kelly, an engineer by training and only the fourth in Gore's history, 'we divide so we can multiply'. How does that work? The Gore organization believes that it can unlock much greater innovation and engagement from its people by keeping smallness. In the mythology of Gore it is said that this was driven by the founder Bill Gore walking around a plant one day in 1965 and realizing he didn't recognize everybody any more. From then on he put in place a principle that no more than 200 people would work in the same building. The company's growth record, enduring innovation and constant presence on 'best company to work for' lists suggests they might have a point.

Even more radical is Gore's lattice structure, which has more in common with networked organizations like Anonymous and the Occupy movement than with the traditional org chart.

In Gore, there are 'few' org charts and 'no chains of command, nor predetermined channels of communication'. So how does work get done? How do people organize themselves? Put simply, how do they manage a multi-billion dollar global business without such structure? As they say on their own website:

'Associates (not employees) are hired for general work areas. With the guidance of their sponsors (not bosses) and a growing understanding of opportunities and team objectives, associates commit to projects that match their skills. All of this takes place in an environment that combines freedom with cooperation and autonomy with synergy.' As CEO Terri Kelly put it in an enjoyable talk at MIT (see link in the Further Reading section) 'Associates vote with their feet'.

Utterly brilliant.

What does the 20th-century manager say to this? 'Pah! Must be like herding cats' and reaches for her latte with a patronizing disdain. Yet when so many organizations complain about their silos and their lack of collaboration, surely a little more fluidity might help? Isn't this how the future looks? People – us – gravitating around the initiatives and projects we feel passionately need to happen?

COACHING

A quick note reinforcing the earlier point about coaching: Gore is small on Management with a capital M, and BIG on coaching. As we'll see later, leadership in Gore is defined by 'followership' – if you don't have an organization mapped out beneath you, what do you have as a manager or leader? Only influence. And every Associate (not employee, as they are keen to point out) at Gore has a Sponsor – that is, someone responsible for their success and usually someone outside of their day-to-day project work. This creates a big coaching culture.

CULTURE EATS BUREAUCRACY FOR LUNCH

In her MIT talk, current CEO Terri Kelly spoke throughout about the tension between the Gore culture and bureaucracy, and how their goal as the environment has become more complex is to keep driving out bureaucracy. Kelly also made the point that 'with the right people, a few clear objectives and guidelines you don't need a lot of rules'.

There is the famous quote from management theorist Peter Drucker that 'culture eats strategy for breakfast'. I propose a second: 'culture eats bureaucracy for lunch'!

NIXONMCINNES

NixonMcInnes is the company that I am part of, and am proud to have co-founded. Each of the following three practices was created by other people in our incredibly talented team – I cannot take the credit, but I can spread the ideas!

CHURCH OF FAIL

At a company away weekend in a farmhouse we'd hired in the Welsh hills, we split into groups to work on the company culture by developing initiatives that would not only benefit our company but also our clients'.

One group designed a little process to work on the idea of celebrating failure in NixonMcInnes. They developed the seed of their idea based on a stagecraft exercise that Matt Matheson in our team had experienced in his improv work to teach novice improvisers to accept applause and become better accustomed to feeling uncomfortable.

Out of this was born Church of Fail: a bizarre but powerful cultural ritual in our little company. Once a month, the boardroom at NixonMcInnes is converted into a non-denominational (!) church – with the chairs laid out in rows, all facing to the front where a sign of paper marks the 'comfort zone'. On the wall behind the congregated audience is a poster with three instructions on it:

1 How did you fail?
2 What did you do about it?
3 What did you learn?

One by one, volunteers – and the whole thing is a little whacky so it definitely has to be voluntary – walk to the front, stand in the comfort zone and, looking at their peers, describe a time that they failed in the last period. Having described their failure, the congregation begin to cheer and clap loudly. It is both incredibly uncomfortable to be stood there at that moment and enormously amusing seeing your colleagues whooping and clapping uproariously at the best (i.e. worst) failure you could remember. As much as the

confessor wants the moment to end, so the applause continues way beyond the point of comfort. And then, when
the group sense enough has been done, it tails off, and so
their turn is done and it is on to the next volunteer.

What we hope this does is change our own perceptions
of failure over time. It is hugely cathartic to socialize your
biggest fail of the previous month in front of your peers,
and I imagine it is good for our people to see all of us –
regardless of our supposed importance or length of service
– stand up and discuss our failures.

COMMUNICATION WORKSHOPS

Another practice that we ran for about 18 months was a
rolling programme of communication workshops. Conceived and delivered by our unique finance director, Lasy
Lawless, who is also a trained therapist (yep, accountant
and therapist, all in one brain) and our wise chairman (now
non-exec) Pete Burden – who has been working with, and
prototyping, progressive business practices his whole career
– these sessions were fairly simple in structure.

The group, again made up of volunteers, sat around
in a circle in a private meeting space (for us, the boardroom). There would usually be ten or so people, and Lasy
or Pete as the facilitator would introduce the basic ground
rules and the 'Three Core Conditions' that we wished to
practise:

■ Respect – for the other person as a human being, regardless of their behaviour.

- Empathy – experiencing the world as another experiences it (putting oneself in the other's shoes).
- Congruence – being appropriately open and transparent about one's own thoughts and feelings.

With these principles in mind we would practise this 'conscious communication', talking as a group about awkward incidents and issues that had come up and how they had made us feel. If it sounds a bit like group therapy, it probably was but I really cannot say as I've never done therapy! (Not yet, anyway).

Over time, the groups fizzled out – I think this was for two reasons: first, that we all found them a bit weird in a work context and the overlap never felt entirely comfortable; and second, that they had to some extent served their purpose – everyone in the team has got better at communicating honestly and authentically. For some people it involves little changes in how they speak and how they listen, and for others it has helped make big improvements in their communication with people at work, particularly under stress. For my part, I learnt lots and am glad we did it. I just need to remember to apply it when the heat is on!

HAPPY BUCKETS!

In the 21st century, one of the obvious challenges for the business community is to measure its contribution in more than financial terms alone. We have seen where a singular focus on the bottom line gets us. However, even for more progressive businesses, there is a prickly challenge – especially when there is greater transparency around the company's finances – which is that the more open the financial data, the more powerful and influential that data can become.

Imagine a company where every Monday morning every single team member is told exactly how much profit/loss the company stands to make that month and that year, how much cash is in the bank and therefore exactly what shape the company's finances are in and what that means to each individual. For better or worse, that is what happens at NixonMcInnes every Monday.

It can be a horrible way to start a week. In our own efforts to balance the financial aspects of the business with other equally vital considerations we measure happiness every day.

Quite simply we have three buckets – one full of tennis balls, and then two buckets which start every new day empty: a happy bucket and an unhappy bucket. These are by the door to our office, and on the way out at the end of each day you pick up a ball and toss it in the bucket that best reflects your day. Simple.

On the door is a sheet, and we fill out the number of happy and unhappy balls every day as the week progresses. Anyone can count them up, it's a pretty straightforward system. And then our office manager adds them to a spreadsheet. We now have happiness data going back to June 2010. (Recently Beth Granter in our team wrote a blog post analyzing that happiness data against our financial performance – see the Further Reading section for a link.)

We believe this matters. We believe that in creating a currency around our mood, we put a marker down – it shows that it matters, it gives us a point of reference for discussions in teams and as individuals. It also provides a powerful self-awareness check: 'why am I putting another ball in the unhappy bucket? What's going on? What do I need to do or who do I need to talk to?'

And, for me as a manager, it's like a spring in the stride or a kick in the gut the minute I walk in the next morning. As I write this on a Sunday morning I see that on Friday we had 30% of balls in the unhappy bucket – that is not normal for a Friday, and I'm now conscious of it. I have realtime feedback about my team's well-being, their mood – and I cannot hide from it. It is ambiently transmitted, for better or worse. It forces me and all of us to act (or at least to consciously choose not to).

So how can you evolve how your organization interacts with its people?

Here are the four areas to explore:

1 Creating strong values and principles
2 Celebrating personality
3 Enabling people development
4 Establishing freedom and trust

1 CREATING STRONG VALUES & PRINCIPLES

Having spent time studying companies that absolutely nail the Progressive People bit, it is clear that one characteristic that they all share is the clarity and belief around their values.

At the WorldBlu Live conference, speaker after speaker from visionary companies outlined their crystal clear values, and what really comes through from organizations like Zappos and Gore are the values that are woven throughout the whole organization: from 'Create Fun and a little Weirdness' at Zappos to 'The ability to make one's own commitments and keep them' at Gore.

So, what are the values that you want to imbue your team with? Or, better, what are the values that together you are willing to stand by, to hold one another to account and to really strive for in your work?

2 CELEBRATING PERSONALITY

In the 20th century, being professional and being yourself were seen as different things. Being professional was not only about delivering against promises made and to a high standard, in other words, about being trustworthy. It was also about being neutral (like the colour of those old beige desktop PCs, again!) and, in doing so, acting within some powerful puritan norms – a little polite laughter, no rough language (at least not at first) and definitely no weirdness. As for emotions, a professional didn't show 'em.

In the 21st century, when the alternative to many knowledge worker jobs is a freelance career, where the alternative to working in an office is working from home or in a co-working space, and in a century where people are realizing that there's more to life than work alone, these notions of professionalism are shifting. Hurrah for a return to personality!

What is clear about these progressive businesses that celebrate people is that they welcome and value personality, authenticity, emotion and humour.

This poses new challenges for us all. At our company we know it usually takes a new team member six months to really become themselves at work. Undoing the brainwashing of bad business takes time. And celebrating personality poses challenges to you as a leader, whichever level you lead from. You must lead. You must be authentic, you must celebrate your own real self at work, and make it OK for others to do the same. Easy to say, difficult to do: particularly on bad days.

So can you start doing this tomorrow? How can you be more 'you' and encourage others to do the same? At scale, how will you institutionalize that? What practices will help it happen?

3 ENABLING PEOPLE DEVELOPMENT

In this chapter there is an underlying constant which is about enabling people to improve themselves. It is not enforced, and it is not limited to the slightly twee 'personal development' that you can find on your local bookshop's shelves. More than that, it is an ethos of allowing and enabling the organization's people to develop themselves both in their professional and especially in their personal aspects.

How does your organization enable real personal development? What can you do to promote development in the people around you?

4 ESTABLISHING FREEDOM AND TRUST

Perhaps the biggest ideas that 21st century organizations embrace are those of freedom and trust. BOOM. Big words, and kinda the diametrical opposite to the established cultures of most businesses. But isn't that what we demand and expect today?

In his fantastic TED talk in July 2009 'Dan Pink on the surprising science of motivation', Pink talks about the three aspects of motivating people as being autonomy, mastery and purpose. We've looked at how the three businesses in this chapter each extend significant trust and freedom to their people, and reap the rewards. In the chapters that follow, freedom and trust are constants. Not overt, but in the background of pretty much everything we go on to look at – from Conscious Leadership right through to the final chapter on Fair Finances.

I guess the question for you is, what can you do with freedom and trust in your organization? Because they feel like the backdrop for and the shortcuts to this whole chapter. It's what it all boils down to. Are you going to actually let them – the people – deliver great things? And who – in your organization – might not, and why not?

ACKNOWLEDGING CHALLENGES

Before finishing this chapter, it would be remiss not to look some of the challenges around people in the contemporary organization. There are three that we look at here:

1 COMPETITION

Competition between peers does not necessarily lessen in a more enlightened business culture. In fact, my current belief is that it may increase.

By opening things up, with greater transparency, less official hierarchy and a culture and practices which create much more feedback inside the organization, it is likely that a ferocious meritocracy is created. 'Great', you may cheer! That may be so, but I believe I am working in such a place and dealing with some of the consequences of an environment where there is both an incredibly strong team ethic *and* very high competition between peers. That is not easy. And, for the team members themselves, it can feel very stressful (alongside being motivating) to be part of an organization where there is a relentless drive towards performance, with few places to hide.

Hearing Gore CEO, Terri Kelly, talking about how every Gore Associate (herself included) is ranked by their peers I cannot help thinking that one of the consequences of some of these 'better' people practices may be a tilt towards unhealthy competition which will need monitoring and counter-balancing.

This is worth looking out for, particularly when team members may be going through a life event or a phase in their life or career that does not naturally thrive in this environment. You may need to be extra vigilant for these people and nurture them through.

2 DROWNING IN FREEDOM AND HONESTY

A related issue can be that, in an organization where there is greater fluidity, less definition around roles, less directive people management and a greater emphasis on feedback, team members can end up becoming overwhelmed.

When there is little structure to hang on to, many opportunities to engage with and a high performing team to fit into, a new employee may end up drowning and become overwhelmed by the lack of structure and huge possibilities that exist. I imagine that at Gore this is a huge part of what the Sponsor provides to a new Associate.

Similarly, a new team member at NixonMcInnes described the environment as 'like having the honesty volume turned up'. (Remember also Namasté's FOH communication.) That can be tough to deal with at first if a person has become accustomed to a less direct, less authentic approach to communication and management information in a different organization.

3   SOME PEOPLE WANT A 20TH-CENTURY JOB

Finally, some people will perhaps *want* a 20th-century job even in the 21st century. Maybe they want to do just what they came in to do, to do the same thing for years, to know little about how they or the organization are doing, and maybe that is OK. These kind of people – and they may even include you – do not want to sit around in a circle talking about their feelings, they do not want some kind of airy-fairy coaching from a 'sponsor' – they want a boss, and they want to be told what to do.

I can identify with that desire. Changing behaviour is really hard. Changing a culture or a group of people's expectations and attitudes about their work is really hard too. Some people are open to change, while others will resist to the bitter end. In his experience making these kind of changes at HCLT, with tens of thousands of employees, CEO Vineet Nayar observed three groups: Transformers, who wanted change; Fence Sitters, who would take a wait-and-see approach; and Lost Souls, who were entrenched and would refuse to move. In *Employees First, Customers Second* Nayar describes how he chose to focus on the Transformers, with the rationale that they would convert those Fence Sitters who were willing to change. Your mileage may vary, and a different approach may suit your team or organization.

Whatever the case, recognizing that many people actually want a 20th-century job is crucial. When the fit is not right, try to spot it early on – the signs will usually be there. In an environment where the individual cannot thrive, they cannot be really happy and they will sap your efforts. Be clear, and be sure to follow through swiftly – not everybody is ready or up for these progressive ways! It's better for them and for you if you recognize and act on that.

SUMMARY

People are the lifeblood of any business. In this chapter, we have spent some time thinking about what it is that contemporary organizations do with their people to create real advantages. And there are many more practices available than those we have been able to cover in this book.

Fundamentally, what it boils down to is beliefs. If you believe that people are the first, the last, and the everything

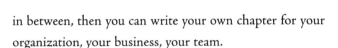

in between, then you can write your own chapter for your organization, your business, your team.

People say that we are in a talent war, and that in business the best team wins. If that is true, then taking these next steps is the difference between whooping ass and being left behind. I know where I'd rather be.

Having looked at Progressive People as a whole in this chapter, we now drill into that fascinating role of leadership in a progressive company.

Further reading

- *Happiness Delivered* by Tony Hsieh
- 'Dan Pink on the surprising science of motivation' TED July 2009 – http://bit.ly/cltrshk5
- Terri Kelly, CEO, W.L. Gore & Associates – http://bit.ly/cltrshk6
- Beth Granter's analysis of NixonMcInnes happiness data and financial performance – http://bit.ly/cltrshk7

CHAPTER FOUR

CONSCIOUS LEADERSHIP

It is quite deliberate that the order of this book puts the topic of people before that of leadership. In fact, it reflects both a switch from the contemporary sequence of leadership first, people second and a return to Julius Caesar's long-standing maxim that 'every soldier has a right to competent command'.

As General Patton put it in his book *War As I Knew It* back in 1947: 'There has been a great deal of talk about loyalty from bottom to top. Loyalty from the top to the bottom is much more important and also much less prevalent. It is this loyalty from the top to the bottom which binds juniors to their seniors with the strength of steel.'

So what defines a 'competent command' in today's environment? And are we at risk of reverting to military models and top-down thinking here? Having understood the challenges and opportunities around Progressive People, maybe it is clear that this contemporary organization demands a substantially different type of leadership. This is an approach that will be hugely welcomed around the world, though it will take time for all of us to adjust and wean ourselves off some of the myths and folklore around leadership.

And is the contemporary leader actually new or is this just a rehashing of principles which have existed for mil-

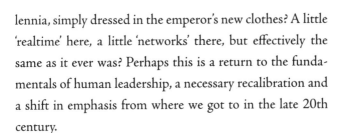

lennia, simply dressed in the emperor's new clothes? A little 'realtime' here, a little 'networks' there, but effectively the same as it ever was? Perhaps this is a return to the fundamentals of human leadership, a necessary recalibration and a shift in emphasis from where we got to in the late 20th century.

THE CHALLENGE OF LEADERSHIP IN THE 21ST CENTURY

The leader in a progressive business is walking a path that many of her peers before her will not have done. She may not be able to get advice as easily, or support from her stakeholders and investors as immediately.

One important note of caution: there is a great deal of folklore around leadership. Many, many books are published every year on leadership, building on an accepted canon of well-established management wisdom. I do not wish to add to that, and particularly not to the idea that leadership is beyond the many, the preserve of a few 'special' people destined to become leaders.

So do not be intimidated by what follows.

You already lead, so you must already be a leader – at different times, and in different domains of your work and your life. Nobody does it well all of the time. Instead, these are ideas and possibilities about how you can continue to develop as a more conscious leader, ever more able to lead in the 21st century; a person who can help lead in a different world, changing their organization, their team and themselves. That is all!

WHAT IS *NOT* CONSCIOUS LEADERSHIP?

Before we look at what leadership needs to become let's think about conventional leadership first. What is wrong with conventional leadership, you may ask. In fact, you probably won't. Because most people hold conventional leaders in pretty low regard these days. A recent study confirming this is the excellent Edelman Trust Barometer which shows big drops in trust for government officials and CEOs (see Further Reading section at the end of this chapter). So let's remind ourselves what leadership has largely become in modern day business and beyond.

In these cynical times, conventional leadership:

- Celebrates analytical and 'factual' rather than emotional and intuitive.
- Holds power rather than distributes it.
- Distributes rewards unfairly, and has a particularly high influence over its own unfair rewards.
- Is not reflective of diversity in the wider population: in gender, ethnicity, sexuality and other types of diversity.
- Can thrive and be highly rewarded despite terrible performance.
- Is disconnected from the realities of its stakeholders, other than customers (sometimes) and investor/owners and the financial community (always).
- Lacks skills in dialogue, influence, creativity, vision and imagination.
- Does not walk their own talk.

- Fundamentally lacks ethics and spine.
- Favours short-term results over long-term investments.

For me, conventional leadership is too male, too top-down, too analytical, too micro-managery, too short-term, too beholden to too few stakeholders. Conventional notions of leadership are basically a bullshit style and approach for the society we live in. In fact, it baffles me that we've tolerated it thus far.

So this *has* to change. Like, absolutely must change. We must change it.

THE BENEFITS OF CONSCIOUS LEADERSHIP

If the behaviour of people in organizations is substantially shifting, then clearly leadership must shift too. Why should we invest in this shift? Clearly there are the benefits of an unleashed and engaged workforce that were outlined in the previous chapter.

On top of this is a higher order of benefit. Can you imagine a world where leadership had transcended and evolved from the good and bad bits we found in the 20th century? Can you imagine the problems that will be solved in the world through the work of a new generation of conscious leaders, working with purpose and vigour? Can you imagine what it will be like to be part of organizations alive with this kind of leadership? That is the prize, that is the why!

And if we can gather and energize a whole generation of progressive leaders, what will the benefits be?

- More organizations working towards Purposes of Significance, leading to a better world for all (seriously!).
- Healthier, happier and more meaningful work lives for millions, if not billions.
- Fairer rewards for all participants in business, leading to a more resilient business community and a healthier society.
- Higher standards and demands for leaders in all walks of lives, and a new set of role models to help inspire and lead the way.
- Greater self-leadership in all.

What incredible potential.

SO WHAT DOES CONSCIOUS LEADERSHIP LOOK LIKE?

Here are seven components of Conscious Leadership:

1 Leading yourself
2 Style
3 Trust and ethics
4 Transparency
5 Rewards
6 Communication/realtime
7 Support

1 LEADING YOURSELF

Just as this book puts people before leadership, we must also put leading ourselves before leading others.

There are many appallingly bleak but recognizable models of management style such as the mushroom management ('keep 'em in the dark and feed 'em crap'), the seagull ('arrive in a flap, squawk around for a while, crap over everybody and then fly out') and so on. We know that they exist because we have all seen and experienced them!

Will those approaches to leadership help organizations thrive in the 21st century? I really don't believe so. So what allows this to happen in the first place? Two things: a lack of organizational awareness and a lack of personal awareness.

As transparency rises in society at large, and inside businesses in particular, more and more feedback will exist openly about manager and leader performance. As the agenda to make boardrooms more transparent and accountable to shareholders and wider stakeholders, again the same forces will drive an openness and awareness previously unseen. The organization will learn more quickly and more transparently what works and who performs, which naturally then must influence the individual leaders and managers. Transparency has a momentum of its own – and will permeate all of our organizations.

As a result, in the evolved organization it will be very hard to lead others unless you are constantly learning, and improving on how you manage yourself. (In fact, that is the case today – it's just a lot of people get away with crap leadership because the world allows them to.)

So knowing how to lead yourself means knowing the answers to the following questions:

- What is my purpose in this work? Why do I want to do it?
- What motivates and demotivates me?
- What are my values, and which ones am I honouring and which am I not honouring in this work?
- What do I believe my strengths and weaknesses are, and how am I consciously working with them?
- What do the people around me believe my strengths and weaknesses are?
- How do I bounce back from challenges and re-energize when I'm low?
- What are my blind spots, what don't I know about myself?
- What do I tend to resist or ignore?

Knowing these answers is an iterative and constant learning process. The answers may change over time, or become more (or less) clear. Knowing to keep reflecting on them, and practicing and evolving methods of operating from these answers is the key to self-leadership. We look at some practices further on in the chapter to help with locating these answers in yourself.

2 STYLE

Just as we are all different, so are our styles and approaches to engaging with people and therefore 'leading'. There is no correct style for this kind of evolved business we look at throughout this book.

However, there are a few stylistic themes or tensions to be aware of. The first is the tension between being the all-solving hero and the convenor or curator of the group.

HEROIC LEADERSHIP

In the popular definition of leadership, the leader rides in on his white stallion, glistening in the midday sun, holding a spear aloft, squinting slightly with a look of hard resolve, his mouth (and this leader definitely is a 'him') is very human, his ears wise, his arms strong, his hands etc. etc. You get the idea. Now that he has arrived, the problem will be solved. Be it through wisdom, strength, bravery or decisiveness, this leader will fix it and in record time! 'Stand back, minions!!! I AM SOLVING THE PROBLEM!'

Personally, I find this style very attractive, and am drawn to it regularly. One of my biggest flaws is that I want to be the hero, the all-fixing leader. If you have the same idea about how you should be as a leader, then you will find that the issue is that it crowds out the possibility for others to participate, for the group to function as a whole, and for others to step up and take responsibility. To unlock a team's full potential through their participation and democratic practices, this style may not be best. To engage an organization of smart, progressive people that have seen through the fallacies of old school leadership, this style may not be best. You may have a different but equally obstructive style – the all-knowing oracle, the hyper-organized micromanager. Think about it.

CONVENING, CURATING, GARDENING

Perhaps a better style to adopt, more of the time, is not that of the hero (or the others you thought of), but of a convener or curator of the group – be that a whole organization or a small team. The shift here is from being the individual fixer that the most complex issues get escalated to, to being the person that helps the group observe what is happening, creates the space for them to share in that information, helps them reach decisions and create accountability.

This is a more removed personal style of leadership than the heroic mode – this is leadership as facilitation or, if you prefer the metaphor, gardening. Adding something here, pruning a little there, encouraging this bit to come forward, digging deeper, patiently nurturing changes and growth.

Given that we are now managing groups of people whose behaviour and attitudes may be becoming more like volunteers, that we are managing people distributed physically (whether they are working from home or working across multiple geographies), and in an environment where the best talent has given up on the idea of a job for life and can pick or choose from the best jobs, our style may need increasingly to become one of influencing rather than directing. Or curating/gardening over heroic leadership.

The challenge for you – and any of us – is that when we are told 'you're in charge', it is easy to assume a directive style. After all, it's a known style – it's what we've been trained in since school. I say 'jump', you say 'how high?' Teacher, boss, captain, coach, general – all of these have had different styles, but the commonly held view is that leadership is about telling people what to do and making sure they do it. As emotionally intelligent types, we probably don't couch it like that – but our inclinations, particularly under stress, will be directive. It is the established paradigm, so no need to explain that. What can be much harder is to resist that model and the indoctrination there, and to overcome the urge simply to tell everyone what to do. The challenge, then, is to influence and persuade, to garden and curate, rather than just to direct.

MANAGING VOLUNTEERS AND CREATING 'FOLLOWERSHIP'

As we have touched on, the people in our organizations will increasingly demand this adapted, evolved style of management. Gen Y in particular seek the dialogue, participation and feedback from their manager, and meaning in the work. Managing Gen Y is often characterized as managing volunteers: finding ways to excite, cajole and generate tangible results from a group of people who have lots to give but will not respond well to being told what to do.

As John Chambers, the long-standing CEO of Cisco put it in an interview with the *New York Times*, in 2009: 'I'm a command-and-control person. I like being able to say turn right, and we truly have 67,000 people turn right. But that's the style of the past. Today's world requires a different leadership style – more collaboration and teamwork, including using Web 2.0 technologies.'

Interestingly, at Gore they talk about leadership being 'defined by followership'. That is, that the group nominates its leaders – they 'vote with their feet' as CEO Terri Kelly puts it. You cannot be a leader at Gore without having people that are willing to follow you. What a powerful evolution from the norm.

So the questions for you are:

- How do you create followership in your work?
- What is it that you do that makes the people around you want to follow you?
- And what is it that you do that makes people *not* want to follow you?
- Finally, if your people weren't paid and were volunteers, how would you engage with them to create the best results possible?

CHANGING STYLES

A quick, common-sense reminder that leadership is situational: there surely will be occasions where this more directive 'heroic' stance is the right one to take. And others where being the curator or gardener will generate the best results for and from the group. That is the judgement we all have to make continuously – which style and approach is right for this context.

3 TRUST AND ETHICS

Underpinning much of the 21st-century approach to a more conscious leadership are trust and ethics, just as trust and freedom underpinned the previous chapter.

The trust dimension is about having the confidence that the people and the practices of the organization will deliver the desired results. Trust is particularly important in helping us accept some of the contemporary practices we talk about in this book: giving power to more of the people in the organization; allowing new spokespeople to emerge; entrusting big decisions to groups rather than making decisions in ones and twos.

Without trust, there can be no empowerment of others – instead, a lack of trust creates a centre of gravity that leads to micromanagement across the whole organization, which in turn creates slowness, bottlenecks, stifles creativity and so on.

So there must be trust flowing from the leaders in the organization. There should be a default 'I trust you' position rather than a default 'I don't trust you'; though in many organizations it feels the other way around.

The final point to make on trust is that the most powerful thing a contemporary leader may do is to publicly fail inside (and outside) the organization. By failing and communicating that failure, leaders make it OK to fail *and* immediately create a different context for trust to exist in. It sets a precedent and provides, at least, the promise that others in the organization can fail too (this is why endeavours like Church of Fail can be so powerful). This is wonderful fuel for the creation of trust, because it powerfully demonstrates that it is OK to be vulnerable in this organization. Leaders fail first. In fact, that's a nice slogan: Leaders fail first.

The ethics dimension is about behaving with integrity – and particularly about doing only what you would be happy the whole world knowing about if that email or decision was shared with the whole world. I'm sure there are great books on this whole topic – do we really need to describe ethics? You might think so, looking at some business people's behaviour. But really, it is just about doing the right thing, all of the time. (Simple!)

4 TRANSPARENCY

Leading in a more transparent world demands different things from us. We can break these into two sub-categories: informational transparency and emotional transparency.

Leaders have always dealt with a higher degree of transparency than everyone else in an organization, to the extent that they have always been highly visible, are subject to higher expectations than normal and are typically surrounded by – and at the centre of – a variety of competing influences and stakeholders. Clearly this varies hugely: from being a manager in a medium-sized organization to being the CEO of a Fortune 500 multinational, or a leading politician.

This transparency has manifested itself in a variety of ways: from gossipy tabloid stories about personal lives through to the fact that executives in publicly listed companies have their remuneration published openly to the whole world.

However, as we continue to discuss in this book, this transparency around information – not only rewards, but also performance, feedback and increasingly other more subtle data (think MPs' expenses, or carbon footprints, or travel patterns) – is going to increase.

So, as a leader, you must prepare for and cope with more and more information about you and your various impacts being open and available to others.

The emotional transparency of the coming age of leadership is perhaps the more demanding shift.

If the organizations that we lead in are becoming more conscious, more authentic and more open to dialogue and listening, then we leaders must necessarily become so too. It will not be possible for the people in an organization to take their risks and become more vulnerable and open at work if the leaders do not lead the way.

Emotional transparency requires leaders to be congruent: to act in accordance with their feelings no matter how unexpected that is. Can you imagine you or other leaders in your organization saying any of the following to a group of your people:

- 'I'm scared about this and I don't know what the answer is'
- 'I'm feeling sad'
- 'I need help, I'm lost right now'
- 'I feel like going home and hiding'
- 'When I look at this, I'm ashamed to be part of this organization'
- 'I feel guilty because I haven't done my job well in this area'

Yes, these statements are deliberately provocative. But what would it be like if people were more emotionally transparent at work, more of the time, and starting with the leaders? What is your biggest fear here, when you read through that list of proposed 'acceptable things for a leader to say'? Are there benefits to this approach? What are the downsides and risks? And how emotionally transparent or 'congruent' are you most of the time?

5 REWARDS

The rewards of leaders in organizations, particularly CEOs and the board, have been at the forefront of media and activist attention for a long time. Hopefully that pressure and attention will continue – it feels like there are some ugly wrinkles, developed in the latter part of the 20th century, that still need ironing out. Wrinkles such as multi-million dollar golden parachutes for failing CEOs, the lack of a relationship between value-creating performance and rewards more generally, the lack of transparency and rigour in the setting of top management rewards including weak or non-existent remuneration committees, and so on. This, however, feels like it is in hand – the world knows about it and expectations and behaviours are gradually changing.

However, there are two additional concerns that fit into the scope of this book: the ratio of rewards for top earners compared to the rest of the workforce; and a shift towards recognizing the value of non-financial rewards.

In a social business, the ingredients of a more empow-ered organization and greater transparency result in a clearer focus on the inter-relationship between people's rewards in the organization. And, in recent times, as the Occupy movement has reminded all of us, the rich have been growing richer and the poor poorer. The gap between the haves and the have-nots keeps on growing. An aware-ness of this has led many progressive businesses to put in place formal ratios or a system of monitoring the ratio

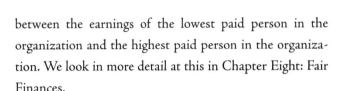

between the earnings of the lowest paid person in the organization and the highest paid person in the organization. We look in more detail at this in Chapter Eight: Fair Finances.

The second concern is that of non-financial rewards. Right now it feels as if most leaders only do it for the money, but there is rapidly growing body of interest around social enterprise, social business (in the Muhammad Yunus definition) and entrepreneurs and leaders doing what they do for a much higher purpose than the accumulation of wealth.

Having looked at motivations in the Progressive People chapter, we have already reminded ourselves that motivation at work is much broader and richer than the pay packet alone. What would it be like if leaders were able to acknowledge the way in which they are nourished by the non-financial rewards of the job are were able to discuss this in a more open and nuanced way?

6 COMMUNICATION/REALTIME

In this networked world, both the demands on and opportunities for leaders around communication are increased. We are living in a world where the time between something of importance happening and the world knowing about it are increasingly the same – the buffer between the two are less and less.

There is less time to prepare the right message. There is less belief and trust in leaders generally, and so in the message itself there is an increased demand for authenticity and honesty. There is an always-on-ness to the world's media, to the workforce with their BlackBerries and internal collaboration platforms (see also Chapter Six: Change Velocity, and Chapter Seven: Tech DNA) so communication cannot be a one-off or occasional piece of work, but more a constant flow.

The combination of these platforms, this growing culture and these expectations is a huge opportunity for all leaders as an outbound communication channel. But there is equal value for leaders in the inbound or dialogue aspect too.

There is a growing application of the concept of 'people as sensors'. In a networked world, there are exponentially more opportunities to harness relevant, timely information, and for people and attention to gravitate towards which sensor has the best available information at any given moment. As Brian Humphrey, then working with the Los Angeles Fire Department, put it in a tweet: 'Every soldier is a sensor. Every citizen is a contributor. Every resident is a reporter of #crisisdata'.

By using the communication landscape to their advantage, contemporary leaders can harness this huge opportunity to plug in to their organizational sensors, and both flow out and flow in realtime information to and from the rest of the business.

7 SUPPORT

The last aspect to leadership in a progressive 21st-century business is putting in place the appropriate support for yourself and other leaders going on this journey.

The world is pretty much geared up to support the 20th-century leader. The expectation is you're a hero and an all-conquering expert, that you're doing it for the money alone, that you do not and will not talk about your feelings (and may not even have them), that you will issue command-and-control dictats from your ivory tower, that you only want to hear good news, that you resist and dislike technology and – probably also – that you're a man or behave like a man and are old and white.

If you are not these, life can be hard. The conventional support networks and the wisdom and advice available through conventional resources may not help you. You may find yourself feeling isolated and stupid – asking yourself 'why am I doing this differently to everyone else – maybe I should stop trying to do things the long, hard, stupid way and just fall in line with everyone else'.

So, to give yourself the best chances of success, you must find or create a support network of people who understand this new world, who belong to the community of changers striving for something different, who have walked the same alternative paths. For me, the single best thing I did on this front was to go to WorldBlu Live 2011 in San Francisco and meet, over the course of three days, a whole community of people motivated by the same things and with many of the same values. It was like coming home! It gave me faith that I wasn't (that) stupid and certainly didn't need to feel like it was only my organization on that path.

Fortunately the world is changing. Our numbers grow! And there are radical shifts in the articles published by the blue-blooded business press (like *Harvard Business Review*), in the newly-celebrated CEO stars (like Vineet Nayar of

HCL) and in the professional support available from accountants, lawyers and associations (like WorldBlu or The Employee Ownership Association).

By addressing and working on these seven dimensions of leadership in the 21st century you will strengthen yourself over time. As you work at it, you will evolve in exciting ways. You will provide a subtle, powerful role model for those around you. You will become the future you want to see in the world.

HOW DO I GO ON THIS JOURNEY?

We can boil these elements down to seven practices, which can help any leader learn and adapt.

1 The Open 360 degree survey
2 Experimentation
3 Sharing personal failures
4 Practising being emotionally congruent
5 Publishing a personal rewards log
6 Using flow tools to share and listen to your team/ organization
7 Building a progressive support network

Let's rattle through the practicalities of each practice.

1 THE OPEN 360 DEGREE SURVEY

This one is awesomely simple and awesomely effective. Take your role description, and put it into an online survey platform like Survey Monkey (or your internal equivalent).

Set it up your survey to have a quantitative section and a qualitative section.

In the quantitative section, configure the survey so that respondents can grade your performance on each area of your role by giving a score (I use 1–5). Results in this section will give you a clear personal benchmark as to how the respondents evaluate your performance and, over time, you can track changes and patterns in the perception of your performance.

In the qualitative section, ask wide open questions designed to give you valuable insights into your performance: your strengths and, vitally, your weaknesses. This section gives you access to real learning from the wise gems that respondents share with you.

I use questions like:

1 What do I do that enables positive performance in the team?
2 What do I do that impairs or reduces performance in the company?
3 What should get more of my time and attention?
4 What three things – if sorted – will substantially improve the company's performance?
5 How can I serve the company better in the next six months?
6 This is just in case there's something extra you want to say or share. You don't need to, it's just for those compelled to say more. I know I'm confusing you now. Sorry.

Before sending this out, you need to talk (ideally face to face) with the people who will be responding. Tell them why you are doing it (clue: to learn!), tell them that you have set it up anonymously because it is about you learning, not about you addressing individual concerns or carrying out a veiled witch-hunt; but if anyone feels compelled to, they can say in the survey who they are. And promise that you will share the high-level results and key takeaways with them – give them a prize and satisfy their curiosity too!

Then send it out, and let the learning begin! You will learn so much about yourself. You may recognize many things, but you may also be shocked or unsettled by others. The important thing, as my colleague Lasy always says, is 'not to swallow the feedback whole'. No one person is 'right' – these are all just many-faceted collages or perceptions of you at work. But, overall, the aggregate will tell you some valuable things.

I recommend doing this once or twice a year. I'm doing mine right now after an 18-month gap due to a shift in annual review cycles at our company, and I am alive with and challenged by the brilliant, gritty, intelligent, on-the-button responses coming back. It's like I'm awake again. Do it. Start today.

2 EXPERIMENTATION

Particularly in the area of styles – which we looked at above – you will need to experiment. You may find through your 360 survey that there are styles you have which create great

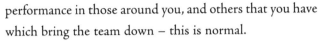

performance in those around you, and others that you have which bring the team down – this is normal.

So, having understood a few of your existing core styles, the goal of experimentation is to expand your range. Try some of the below for size and see how they feel to you and how your people react:

- Relentlessly detail-oriented
- Laid back, bigger picture, dreamy and visionary
- Energetic and bouncy ball of sunshine
- Quiet and pensive professor
- Shouty desk-slamming hardballer
- All-conquering warrior-heroine
- Cheerleading supporter-in-chief and champion of others – 'you can do it!'

Again, where possible it may help to be open about this – to let your people know that you are learning and developing and part of that is about experimenting with styles that are different to your usual two or three default modes.

By the way, what are your default modes? And which styles would you like to add to the range?

3 SHARING PERSONAL FAILURES

Failure is good. All of the research says that to create and innovate we must be prepared to fail and to do so many times. From these failures flow the crucial learning and feedback that helps us succeed. Yet in most organizational cultures failure is toxic, and largely avoided. Real leadership, therefore, is about leading the way in failing, in socializing failure, in making failing OK.

This is simultaneously the easiest and the hardest practice to do. It really is this simple: tell your organization about it when you screw up. You can start small if that helps – it might help the people around you to adjust too! Using the Church of Fail practice outlined in Chapter Three: Progressive People will also provide a powerful and shared platform on which to do this.

You can also use some of the platforms that we look at in the Chapter Seven: Tech DNA to regularly ping out failures (and successes!) without too much pomp and ceremony. In doing so, you normalize failure. This is not *seppuku* (or it shouldn't be) – it is about demonstrating that failure is normal, that it is a huge learning opportunity, and that if the organization and individuals in it are not failing, then they cannot be doing their jobs because they are not learning and not taking risks. Keep that in mind: you're doing the right thing and it will help the organization.

4 PRACTISING BEING EMOTIONALLY CONGRUENT

This is another challenging practice that is sometimes easier to talk about than it is to do. The benefits of being more congruent more of the time are that you will create a more empathic culture, which will lead to less stress for all (including you) because people will not be bottling up their emotions; a more robust and resilient workforce thanks to healthier inter-relationships; and greater performance and

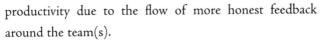

productivity due to the flow of more honest feedback around the team(s).

There's lots more to this topic that we do not have time for, and which is way beyond my level of expertise. However, an appropriately straightforward entry point to doing this, which we have found very useful in our company, is to preface statements with 'I feel . . .'. It's like a hack for the mind, and gets you straight into accessing some of the feelings related to the topic of discussions rather than letting your emotions come out accidentally through the other 99 per cent of your communication (i.e. your body language).

So you say:

'I feel disappointed' rather than 'This is crap'

'I feel amazed'

'I feel delighted'

'I feel incredibly annoyed'

5 PUBLISHING A PERSONAL REWARDS LOG

The British journalist and activist George Monbiot recently began publishing his own Registry of Interests completely voluntarily. As he says himself, 'I have opened this registry because I believe that journalists should live by the standards they demand of others, among which are accountability and transparency. One of the most important questions in public life, which is asked less often than it should be, is "who pays?"'

Is there a way you can do the same? It may be impossible. It may even be a sackable offence! So it's probably worth checking your contract, but if you are an entrepreneur or the CEO, you can make this happen.

6 USING FLOW TOOLS TO SHARE AND LISTEN TO YOUR TEAM/ORGANIZATION

In Chapter Seven: Tech DNA we look at platforms including those we call 'flow tools'. These are the same kind of tools that John Chambers referred to earlier in this chapter – things like Yammer and blogging – which are less formal and much quicker than other traditional communication channels available to a leader or manager.

This is not technology for technology's sake. You don't have time for that. Using these tools is a powerful way to demonstrate to your team or organization the need for, and value in, moving in realtime. The benefit is that by participating you not only show the way and make it OK for others, but also yourself gain access to a realtime pulse of what is happening inside the organization.

7 BUILDING A PROGRESSIVE SUPPORT NETWORK

Finally, you cannot do this alone. You need a support network, and one made up of people that understand all of this. As a leader, no matter at what level in an organization, there are times when you inevitably feel isolated or need the support of those outside your team. If the only kind of support you have is the slash-and-burn or command-and-control management, 20th-century style, then it will be hard to see through these challenging personal changes.

Find people to support you. Put yourself in places where they may come out of the woodwork. Share these ideas so that others might come on the journey and so become part of your network too. Get involved with organizations like WorldBlu, The Employee Ownership Association (UK), National Center for Employee Ownership (USA), and others.

It will be much easier with the right kind of support.

JUST ONE MORE THING

Other practices we have looked at in previous chapters can support you too: remember the Purpose book recommendation, Coaching as a tool for self-awareness, and the Church of Fail and 'Ask Anything' practices to help build trust.

SUMMARY

In this chapter we have looked at the role of leadership in 21st-century business, and broken that role into two lists of seven: seven components of conscious leadership and seven practices to help develop your 21st-century leadership muscles.

This journey towards better leadership is absolutely a journey. It requires change – and change is incredibly demanding. It demands you to get out of your comfort zones; to experiment and, necessarily, to fail; to do things that the people around you find counter-intuitive or even downright odd. And during this journey, especially at times of stress, it will be normal to default to old ways.

But the prize is magical, poetic and brilliant: to become a better leader; to be the change you want to see in the world; to help others see different and better ways of behaving in business. That prize is worth the effort.

If you can lead in these ways, you will be providing a powerful service to more than just your organization – you will genuinely be helping make the world we live in better. Because it is only through significant change, led by leaders at all levels, that we will solve the problems that need solving in the world.

Join us. Come on the journey, and bring your people, your organization. Let's burn yesterday and make a better future for all!

FURTHER READING

■ 'In a Near-Death Event, a Corporate Rite of Passage', Adam Bryant, 1 August 2009, *New York Times* – includes John Chambers quote http://nyti.ms/cltrshk8
■ Edelman Trust Barometer – http://trust.edelman.com/
■ Journalist George Monbiot's personal registry of interests – http://www.monbiot.com/registry-of-interests/

CHAPTER FIVE

ORGANIZATIONAL OPENNESS

Having spent time exploring Purpose, Empowerment, People and Leadership in the first four chapters it is time for us to look into the inherent qualities of progressive organizations – tangible characteristics like Change Velocity, Tech DNA, Fair Finances and starting first with Organizational Openness.

The world we now live in is radically more open than that which existed even five years ago. With the digitization of information, our society is only beginning to scratch the surface of what it is to live in a world where openness is easy and increasingly the default. Do you remember the first time you were sent an email you shouldn't have seen? Who can forget that urban myth of Claire Swire and her email to her boyfriend? With the prevalence of Facebook, incidents like these happen every minute of every day across continents and hundreds of millions of active users. We are still coming to terms with the incredibly low-friction and massively high reach of sharing in the age of the internet, even today.

Wikileaks releases top secret government records, journalists are able to nobble media empires and Members of Parliament through careful and persistent chasing down of digital information. Hacktivists Anonymous expose the names of visitors to paedophilia websites and hack Iranian government email systems. Videos of rogue employees misbehaving at work go around the globe in minutes, amongst billions of hours of video footage of kittens, double-rainbows and other oddities and extreme events that transcend themselves to become popular 'memes', ending up on T-shirts and in popular parlance.

And our young people are growing up in an age where they may have thousands of friends in social networks, a digital footprint of hundreds of photos since they were babies that have been published in some form on the internet without their permission, creating new norms and new behaviours which have older generations shocked at the lack of privacy.

On the plus side, this new, more open world offers benefits we have quickly become accustomed to: we can look up user-generated reviews of the restaurants we plan to eat in, the hotels we plan to stay in, of the tradespeople we plan on hiring to work in our homes. We can learn from other parents in Mumsnet, from other car-lovers in Pistonheads, from other gardeners and genealogists and learners and whoever else we seek, in the ecosystem of niche communities that create a flow of open, helpful information that could never have existed before.

Hard-edged corporations too, even those with the glossiest of brands such as Proctor & Gamble and Lego, have begun to share their most troubling and tricky business problems through crowdsourcing platforms and innovation marketplaces to collaborate and co-create solutions with networks of independent problem-solvers and customers alike.

Why is the progressive business more open?

First and foremost, it makes sense for a progressive business to be more open because openness itself is irresistible. We cannot stop this trend, we cannot hold back this tide, so surely and inevitably we must instead celebrate and harness it.

That may be a little too based on faith alone. Businesses that are inherently more open cannot be driven simply because of some far-off understanding that one day the world will be more like this, can they? There must be some shorter-term reward, something more imminent, more pressing, more rewarding, sooner. There must be for openness to be a powerful part of this radical business movement.

In fact, by being more open, a social business opens up tremendous new opportunities for itself, its people, its customers and wider stakeholders. These benefits include:

- More powerful commitment and smarter problem-solving internally thanks to greater openness around information and performance internally.
- Lower cost and higher impact marketing through the sharing of valuable information from the inside of the organization to the wider world.
- Drastically lower-cost R&D through innovative and blended approaches to creation.

- Serendipity and unexpected consequences from outsiders making connections and creating possibilities where the organization could not see or make them (not only in 'innovation' but in progress and activity generally).
- Reduced costs and massively increased consumer loyalty and word-of-mouth buzz by capitalizing on the trend towards greater participation between creator and consumer, including crowdsourcing, co-creation, crowdfunding and so on.
- And, as a result of all of these, substantially reduced risks through being better prepared and more able to cope in an open world, which in turn creates a competitive advantage over slower, more reluctant competitors.

To understand how contemporary organizations are more open, we need to look at nine distinct areas of openness.

THE NINE AREAS OF ORGANIZATIONAL OPENNESS

1 Culture and behaviour
2 Work environment
3 Systems
4 Innovation
5 Environment issues
6 Marketing and communications
7 Finance
8 Privacy
9 Competition

1 Culture and behaviour

To discuss openness meaningfully, we need to start with your (or any) organization's culture and behaviour. There's a reason why this book is called *Culture Shock*, and that is because so many of the adaptations that need to happen and the opportunities that are available are cultural. The following six domains on this list all interact with culture – they create it and they are created by it, they are all inter-linked. But culture is like the glue binding them all together, which is why it is first.

So what does an open culture look like? Here's a check-list; as you read through it, think about your own organization and where you are.

In an open culture:

- Almost all information is available to almost all members of the organization – there are few secrets and it is easy to get the information you need.
- People across the whole organization are open about their emotions – there is little disguising or hiding of true feelings.
- Collaboration is a natural state, both within distinct organizational structures (like teams and divisions) and across them – there is little evidence of silos and no problem with people hoarding knowledge and protecting turf.
- The organization collaborates as well as competes with its competitors – there is a nuanced view that competitors are also valuable collaborators who help build the market and ongoing joint projects.

2 WORK ENVIRONMENT

Interestingly, the trend towards openness is also affecting our organizations internal environments, and is beginning – along with other trends over the past decades like those of global competition and the associated pressures for some companies to drive down costs in order to compete – to transform how our workspaces look and operate.

Some of the emerging elements of these changing working environments include:

■ A shift from closed offices and cubicles to more shared spaces. Increasingly organizations are re-designing their spaces to have more 'third spaces' as Starbucks described themselves – that is, casual, comfortable, collaborative spaces like coffee shops, sofa areas and open-plan spaces suited to informal meetings and conversations.

■ A shift from fixed desk spaces for all towards more hot-desking and even co-working. For several decades this has been happening, and many people have experienced both the pluses and the minuses of hot-desking. The next iteration of this trend is co-working: collaborative, shared workspaces for freelancers, independents and distributed employees who would otherwise work from home or alone in solo office spaces. What is particularly interesting about co-working spaces is how they physi-cally design-in the opportunities for cross-over, seren-dipity and formal collaboration that we look at in the area of innovation (discussed further down this list). In a co-working space, an architect sits next to a web developer, who sits across from a medical instruments sales rep, who shares a desk space with their illustrator partner. Co-working is the physical manifestation of a blended, connected, loosely related workforce.

■ A shift from 'the company provides the best technology' to an emerging 'bring your own' approach. Not long ago, the technology at work was pretty good and often better than that which most of us had access to at home. Over the past decade, that balance has inverted – many employees in developed and developing countries have better technology in their pockets and their home-offices than they are made to use at work! We are just starting to see intelligent organizations moving to harness this trend, with an emerging movement towards 'here's your tech budget, here's an approved list of technology that will play nice with company systems – go choose the tools that are best for you and your job'.

■ A shift from company firewalls preventing access to large chunks of the web to an opening up of permission and a corresponding move towards IT as enablers rather than policers. When I worked in a traditional business in my first and (so far) only 'proper' job, it quickly became obvious that IT were gatekeepers. Theoretically there to serve the organization, the IT manager wielded an unusual amount of power and seemed to revel in making things difficult. As an aside, he meant well, and did actually wear Disney ties – some stereotypes are true! Fortunately, times have changed in some organizations and there are those in IT who see themselves not only as

gatekeepers and managers of security, but also as enablers of business results. As a result, in some organizations there is an enlightened recognition that employees
need access to almost all of the web in order to carry out
their lives and often to do their jobs too. As the excellent
author and consultant Euan Semple puts it: 'Banning
social sites at work is for wimps – real managers have
conversations with their time wasters about wasting
time'. That's where we need to get to. The 'bring your
own' tech approach above is also a pretty enlightened
trend. Long may the shift from IT as police to enablers
continue! We look at this in more detail in Chapter
Seven: Tech DNA.

3 SYSTEMS

Do you remember when Google Maps first came into your
world? Suddenly, Google Maps was everywhere. It was the
backdrop for news items on TV as the presenter introduced a piece about Iraq or Iowa – there was this big fat
satellite-type map and, in the corner, the Google Maps
logo. It was soon popping up on other organizations' websites – there, in the middle of an otherwise branded web
page, was a Google Map of their office location. And then
entirely new services popped up, plotting all sorts of interesting property or crime or weather data onto a map that
just happened to be a Google Map.

What Google did so brilliantly was to build openness
into the heart of their Google Map product. This was a
map that came with a plug and a set of rules that said 'hey,

as long as you follow these rules, you can come along and plug into me and have a Google Map as part of your service and for free'.

You see, somewhat fascinatingly, for non-technical geeks like me who are attracted to shiny cool technologies that do really useful things, openness, if allowed to, reaches into the very guts of a progressive organization. It goes beyond the culture and the office layout into the very fundamentals of a business, into its systems and its inner core.

This is a huge and unstoppable trend, so let's look at some of the core opportunities.

APPLICATION PROGRAMMING INTERFACE (API)

Although Application Programming Interface isn't the most user-friendly name it does do what it says on the tin from a technology perspective. I think of an API as a plug available in Company A (as with the Google Maps example, or Facebook), which allows Companies B, C, and D to come along and plug into Company A and access some of the core functionality it provides. Simply put, this allows Companies B, C and D to get a lot more done with massively less resources – 'hey, we don't need to create a whole map thing now – we just plug into Google Maps for that part of our new property search engine'. And it allows Company A to substantially increase the distribution of their offering and their brand, and to build competitive advantage through having an ecosystem of related services that build on top of their own, but at little additional cost to themselves (Company A, that is).

This is how – in simple terms – independent companies are producing apps and games used daily by millions inside Facebook. Facebook provides the platform, the plug and the rules. Independent companies are then able to develop their apps and games to take advantage of Facebook's gigantic user base, its user information, its login functionality – the whole damn thing! In theory, everyone wins. Zynga, producers of Farmville, Mafia Wars and Words With Friends, did $600m revenues in 2010 – a huge proportion of which was from game playing happening inside Facebook.

APIs tend to favour companies that have distinct, systematized products and services, and those which are powered by databases and technology – at least at first glance. So organizations providing very tailored products and services may struggle to identify opportunity here. But Facebook and Google Maps may be poor examples to use, because they allow the rest of us in non-digital native companies to get off the hook. That may be a little too easy. This is a seismic shift in how – from a systems point of view – business gets done in the networked 21st century. It will come knocking at the door of your organization and market sooner or later.

To find an opportunity, the way to think about the value that an API strategy can create is to think 'What is the very core of our organization? What are the crown jewels, and how could we accomplish our goals better by allowing other organizations (or individuals) to plug into a carefully considered part of those jewels in a way that creates value for us and for them?'

OPEN DATA

Let's look at an overlapping opportunity, but from a consumer's point of view.

What would it be like if your bank could give you not only your balance and your recent transaction information, but could also provide a dashboard that gave you a sense of the trends in your personal finances and some meaningful insights into patterns and quirks that allowed you to better understand and manage your money?

What would it be like if your car could help you understand what your driving is like, particularly when your driving style is more or less economical (financially and environmentally), when that tends to be in your journeys and why, and what you can do about it?

And, avoiding the old cliché of the internet fridge, would it be helpful if you could Google for your keys when you misplaced them at home (seriously, how cool will that be?), and if you could look up your cat flap data to tell whether the cat was in or out? Increasingly, objects are becoming connected to the internet. The next generation of the web – the Semantic Web – is often popularly characterized as 'The Internet of Things'. Soon it won't just be people and data connected to one another through the web: almost everything will be connected.

In this digitized world, we are all leaving trails of bread-crumbs behind us that are being collected by the companies and organizations providing services to us. Recognizing this, there is a whole raft of innovation happening around the idea of unlocking existing data stores to give value back to the creators – that is, the consumers and users – of that data. Some people are calling these 'data handbacks', and you can see this trend also located in the rise of visualizations of data, in infographics being used in the media to convey complex information through images as well as many other newly spawned opportunities.

Many banks and financial services institutions are beginning to hand back useful intelligence to their customers through a raft of 'Personal Finance Managers' – a good example for further research is Mint.com. The car example I gave just a moment ago is actually the Fiat 500 Eco-Drive which does exactly that – provides useful web-based information, nicely visualized, to the owners of their cars to help them understand and improve their driving.

Here's a business-to-business example: Zappos, who we looked at earlier, has a vendor extranet where the 1000-or-so suppliers that it buys its many lines of shoes from can login and monitor the various stock levels for the lines that they supply. Nothing too revolutionary there, though I'd bet many companies wouldn't allow their suppliers to do the same based on attitudes rather than technology limitations. But what about this? Zappos then permits those 1000-or-so vendors to raise purchase orders from Zappos to them to order new stock where they feel it is necessary.

Let me play that back to you: the supplier raises an order from its customer to buy more stuff from itself, when it wants to. Zappos sees this as 'a thousand extra people helping us to manage our business'. Pow!

So the question for you is: What information do you hold that could be enormously valuable to your customers, employees and stakeholders? And think about it good: there's gold in them thar hills.

4 INNOVATION

Perhaps the most radical influence of organizational openness has been in the way businesses innovate in the late 20th and now early 21st century.

CROWDSOURCING INNOVATION

In 2010, a Russian by the name of Yury Bodrov solved twelve, well-paid, tricky 'challenges' for businesses around the world that he may never need to physically meet. That problem-solving feat made Yury the top solver of the year on innovation marketplace Innocentive. Yury is prolific – the next solver on the year's leaderboard solved four challenges. And the challenges were not posted by just any old businesses: challenges have been set on Innocentive by P&G, NASA, Lilly and Roche.

You can think of Innocentive as a dating website where companies with business problems that need solving can advertise their unfulfilled wishes to talented specialists who love solving problems. Solvers might be passionate soloist 'amateurs' working from their garden shed or a local lab, or

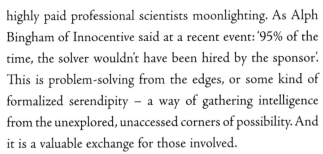

highly paid professional scientists moonlighting. As Alph Bingham of Innocentive said at a recent event: '95% of the time, the solver wouldn't have been hired by the sponsor'. This is problem-solving from the edges, or some kind of formalized serendipity – a way of gathering intelligence from the unexplored, unaccessed corners of possibility. And it is a valuable exchange for those involved.

At Threadless, community members submit new T-shirt designs, community members vote for their favourite designs which then go into production and community members send in photos of themselves and their friends wearing the T-shirts, which Threadless then adds to the product pages. So which bits of the typical T-shirt business does Threadless actually do? Well it prints the T-shirts, it takes some nice photos of them when they are first ready to be purchased, it takes the money and it sends them out – the logistics. But it's just a hobby business though, right? Although the company doesn't disclose financials often, it is in the public domain that Threadless turned over $30m in 2009.

These kind of collaborative, online problem-solving endeavours have been called crowdsourcing – the idea of harvesting or sourcing effort and intelligence from an online crowd or community.

This great opening up has been a radical shift in the way innovation gets done in some organizations.

Previously, innovation was a matter for the Research & Development department. In-house talent would cook up the new product developments, and great innovation factories like 3M (sticky notes!) and Proctor & Gamble (the Swiffer!) would churn them out. This was both a practical reality and a source of company pride.

In this networked age, however, the opportunities to solve problems are far greater. As we have already touched on, businesses are no longer limited by their own available equipment, time, talent and resources. By opening up their fortress walls, these organizations are able to draw on talent dotted around the globe, on ideas and problem-solving approaches that have not (and perhaps would not have) emerged inside their own four walls and so can get better quality solutions to problems, and more quickly.

It's as if businesses have begun to get over the idea of themselves as the be-all-and-end-all and found a new humility. That, or the economics of crowdsourcing is deeply compelling to profit-driven businesses in a hyper-competitive marketplace!

Getting stuff done in government

As governments and local authorities grapple with their delivery challenges in the recent austere, harsh economic environment, they too are exploring how opening up both their resources (like data stores) and their workloads to distributed groups can help. This is not crowdsourced innovation in the mode of Innocentive, but more like crowdsourcing-as-innovation.

Launched in 2009 by Hillary Clinton, the 'Virtual Student Foreign Service' is a US Department of State programme harnessing 'technology and a commitment to global service among young people to facilitate new forms of diplomatic engagement.'

The VSFS pairs 'e-interns' it has recruited – all of whom are American students – with State department offices and US diplomatic posts worldwide, whom they then help with a variety of tasks from their own college and university campuses around the world.

As the VSFS says on its website: 'Past projects asked students to:

- Develop and implement a public relations campaign using social media sites like Facebook, Twitter, MySpace, YouTube, etc. to communicate and reach out to youth.
- Conduct research on the economic situation, prepare graphic representations of economic data, and prepare informational material for the US Embassy website.
- Create a system to gather and analyze media coverage on a set of topics including environment, health, and trade.
- Research IT-based interventions that have been successful in higher education, particularly in teacher training.
- Write and contribute biweekly articles to the US Embassy's Facebook page on topics such as internet, computer science/technology, history, and literature.
- Develop a series of professional instructional video clips to be published by the US Embassy.
- Survey social media efforts of US diplomatic posts, NGOs, and private companies around the world to help

establish best practices in a US Embassy's social media outreach business plan.'

A global workforce of unpaid, willing volunteers? Seems to work for the US State Department in these lean times. If you think back to the 16 basic desires theory – it is these powerful underlying human motivators which make this tick.

SMALLER STEPS IN CROWDSOURCING

However, the big, developed end of crowdsourcing that we have looked at above is increasingly well understood. There are whole books and events and – as we've seen – innovation marketplaces enabling this wonderful connectivity between those with something they need and those with something to give.

What else is there to enable Innovation in progressive businesses around crowdsourcing? There are a couple of fairly simple trends worthy of our attention, both building on the concept of the organization having porous edges so that ideas can flow in and out.

Firstly, hackdays. Hackdays is a wonderfully simple and useful phenomenon to emerge from the developer community. Like any community, software developers have always been drawn to one another and have a rich history of meetups and big community events where they can get together, geek out and make stuff. At hackdays, developers, designers and creatives get together – usually at a weekend – to 'hack' something together: that is, to make something, and usually something they personally believe in – something that scratches an itch they have. Barcamps – a global network of open, user-generated conferences – really helped distribute the methods and benefits of hackdays to a global audience.

We are now seeing the rise of niche-focused hackdays, either around a cause, a specific niche area or around a technology. Organizations are also increasingly using hackdays either to foster innovation internally or externally, as with the recent Honda Hackday in London.

Social Innovation Camp is another brilliant example. It was founded by a few good-spirited, frustrated people in London who felt that there was a huge opportunity to innovate more to provide better practical solutions to social issues in society that just were not being taken up by government, charities and NGOs. The Social Innovation Camp guys felt passionately that some of the making and getting-stuff-done-ness of the hackday formula could usefully be brought to bear on the job of innovating around social causes. The first Social Innovation Camp was run in London in April 2008.

In the UK alone, Social Innovation Camps have generated more than 450 ideas, of which over 30 have been protoyped into social ventures, and a few have continued to grow-including MyPolice, 'an online feedback system for the police service, allowing direct, open conversations between the public and the police', and the awesomely practical SimpleCRB which provides 'a cheaper, quicker and more effective CRB checking service for organizations in the voluntary and public sector'. Real outcomes. Social Innovation Camp has now spread far beyond London alone: camps have happened in Nigeria, South Korea, Australia, Slovakia, Georgia, Czech Republic, Azerbaijan, Armenia, Kyrgyzstan and Bosnia. These lightweight, open movements are so much more viral than their centralized predecessors – they spread.

Second, and perhaps most simple of all, one of the most practical trends around this growing porosity in the edges of organizations is the rise of formats that bring guest speakers and potential collaborators into the organization. Driven by the rise of the great talks available from inspiring events like the TED and TEDx series and the wonderful DO Lectures in Wales, there seems to be a growing consciousness that the world is full of interesting and alarmingly talented people that, if we're not careful, we may never hear from.

At NixonMcInnes we operate a First Friday programme where we simply ask interesting people we know to come on the first Friday of each month and talk to us about their work. I think we 'borrowed' the idea from the fabulous Interesting event in London which gathers together seemingly unrelated but interesting people to talk about their ideas and work. Whilst this kind of thing has been happening for donkey's years, it feels to me that this is now part of something different. Ideas seem to be gaining in currency, and the phenomenal reach of the internet is spreading them further and wider. Just TED alone has – for me – created a new global awareness of the power of ideas. So whilst, for many years, organizations have invited in inter-esting people to talk, perhaps I am suggesting a democratiz-ing of this – a more every day, every-organization opening up happening. If every small and large organization opens their boundaries by one per cent and welcomes in one per cent more of the outside world, what will that do to our whole business community? And why wouldn't we all do that?

5 ENVIRONMENT ISSUES

As we all wake up to the huge environmental challenges ahead of us, so the role of businesses in the creation and solution of those challenges quite rightly comes into focus. In fact, if there is any reason why we need business to evolve, it is to address the environmental challenges we have ahead of us.

Openness will play a substantial role here: governments and activists will continue to use visibility and profile to influence businesses to change and, as the world takes the environment more seriously, this will be increasingly impactful; and secondarily, progressive businesses that make changes sooner than their competition (whether driven by a Purpose of Significance or in response to the influences and changes in their market) will promote their strengths and gain competitive advantage.

CARBON DISCLOSURE PROJECT

An example of this is the Carbon Disclosure Project, a brilliant and well-connected organization headquartered in London with regional offices around the world that 'launched to accelerate solutions to climate change and water management by putting relevant information at the heart of business, policy and investment decisions'. In other words, using the power of organizational openness to drive a change in the behaviour of corporations. CDP creates this openness by inviting businesses to complete an annual questionnaire about their emissions, water management and climate change strategies.

Responding to the questionnaire is voluntary but one of CDPs great insights has been that a failure on behalf of businesses to manage these aspects of their operations would represent a threat to their future business success, in a world where a business that is not environmentally sustainable will become a business that is not economically sustainable. In doing so, CDP has gained the interest of the institutional investment community who increasingly demand that the corporations which they invest in begin to positively manage the sustainability of their business. As such, CDP creates demand from the investors for transparency from the companies which they have shareholdings in. This, in turn, drives up the profile and importance of such information inside the businesses.

WALMART

Whereas CDP could be said to be operating from the top down, there are also initiatives driving greater openness and transparency around environmental impacts, which are bubbling from the bottom up. One such initiative is

Patagonia's Common Threads programme, which we looked at earlier. Another, which has had a huge impact on the sustainability of its business, is Walmart's massive moves towards becoming a greener business.

Amongst an interesting and positive heap of initiatives it has created since 2005, perhaps the most open of its sustainable practices has been the creation of Sustainable Value Networks. As Walmart says on its website: 'SVNs bring together leaders from our company, supplier companies, academia, government, and non-governmental organizations (NGOs.) Together, we explore challenges and develop solutions that benefit our business, as well as our local and global communities.'

Effectively, the SVNs are a vehicle to allow Walmart to invite in some of its biggest critics from activist groups and NGOs, bring in brains and perspectives from academia and government, and also – vitally – draw in its supply chain too. These networks have the responsibility and scope, simultaneously and substantially, to reduce the environmental impact of Walmart business *and* drive down costs in the business. The range is broad: SVNs span in focus from Greenhouse Gas to Chemical Intensive Products.

The brilliance of Walmart's SVNs is their configuration – this really is openness at work, the opening up of a single-organization's 'monoculture' to greater diversity of ideas and values. By following this path Walmart can increasingly see itself less as a traditional company and more as a community where different perspectives are not just tolerated but celebrated.

6 MARKETING AND COMMUNICATIONS

In the famous words of comedian Bill Hicks at a stand-up gig 'if anyone here is in advertising or marketing, kill yourself'. He continues: 'You are Satan's spawn, filling the world with bile and garbage'. Marketing and communications has a huge opportunity in the 21st century, and it is not just to cease being Satan's spawn!

Unfortunately, too often, those in marketing and PR were the creators of opacity – obfuscating and obscuring simple, easy-to-access truths like the fat or salt in a food product, or the true cost of a financial services product, or coaching the CEO to evade difficult questions in interviews, instead droning away at their key messages, disrespecting their interviewers and their audiences.

Alternatively, marketing has been too late and too lacking in influence to substantially improve the given product or service: it has been the recipient of the finished article, told only to 'get it out there' and so it has lobbed freshly packaged products over the corporate wall, bombarding those on the other side with a hail of incoming messages. 'INCOMING!'

What is more, marketers stand accused of creating aspirational expectations for the average Joe that leave him or her feeling miserable with what they really have. They – the argument goes – created the demand for the shiny car, the puffy lips and the orange skin, for the expensive mountain bikes (plural), the two foreign holidays a year. Which led in turn to the spiral of over-borrowing, of credit card debt and general financial woes.

Marketing in the last century was an industrialized process of shoving stuff into the world. There wasn't a great deal of dialogue, there wasn't a great deal of participation and there wasn't – by the end of the century – a great deal of love or respect for Marketing with a capital M. In this mode, marketing was the telling of a tightly controlled story at industrial scale.

That ethos of marketing will not cope with the challenges and changes of the 21st century. It just won't pass. The opportunity for marketing today is in harnessing this momentum towards greater openness. The opportunity is for the stories that organizations tell about themselves and their work to become more authentic, and for their brand to be the aggregate of those – not a sterile but highly polished artefact.

Here are just a few examples of how.

CUSTOMER SERVICE AS MARKETING

In an open and connected world, consumers' and businesses' experiences of the products and services they buy are no longer isolated. There is no longer a kind of asymmetry in the power between the provider and the consumer because, as you will know well, within minutes of finishing a meal – or even during, if you so wish – you can leave a review of a restaurant that will be findable through Google. The power is more balanced now: if tens of customers have bad experiences of a tradesperson or a lawyer, or if tens of thousands of businesses have bad experiences of an energy company or a government department, they can interlink, aggregate into a more formidable whole and distribute 'the truth' about company X far and wide.

This creates a new imperative for marketers, which I believe is already making business better: the imperative to take customer service more seriously than ever before.

As such, customer service is an integral part of the new marketing.

The winning marketers will celebrate the potential of reviews, they will create word-of-mouth through outstanding customer experiences, they will create cultures and processes that imbue their employers with customer-centricity. They will lead each element of the organization to appreciate its role in the customer's end experience. And, as they do, brands will rise and fall based on their transparent, openly available customer service experiences.

OPENNESS AS MARKETING

Secondly, beyond customer service alone, marketers will find ways to create value and advantage from openness in how their organization communicates and interacts with the outside world.

Two simple examples of this are: Skittles and Econsultancy

Skittles, the American candy brand, and Econsultancy, the global marketing membership organization, don't have many characteristics in common. One is B2C, a 'food' business, while the other is B2B and a publishing and community business. But both have experimented with the power of openess in their marketing by transparently displaying tweets about their brand names on their own homepages.

During their now-famous campaign, Skittles turned its whole website homepage over to tweets from people – anyone – mentioning the word 'skittles' in their 140 character update. The result was a minimally-filtered stream of consciousness from a global audience of Skittles lovers, haters and people playing an old-fashioned game of bowling! The rationale here is: 'we are what people say we are – and we're bold enough to project what they say about us on our own sparkly website'. Econsultancy continues to do this to this very day: across their popular marketing resource website (but no longer on the homepage) is a stream of recent tweets mentioning the brand.

Crowdsourcing as marketing

Kickstarter is an incredible exemplar of what is possible with openness in marketing. Kickstarter is a platform where I – a creative – can outline a project I'd like to bring to life: a film I'd like to shoot, a book I'd like to write, a technology I'd like to develop. After describing my would-be project, I can invite the world to become 'backers' – that is, to co-fund the development of the project in return for a small reward – a signed copy of the book for $25 or a private reading for $250!

Some projects are hugely over-subscribed – those that 'go viral' and are passed through social networks as must-help projects, whilst others just meet their targets and some don't at all. The crowd decides, and the crowd funds: this is crowdfunding.

Given that established marketing practice concentrates on research, focus groups, test marketing and piloting and so on, why won't this kind of early-stage openness and participation become mainstream marketing in the development of products and services? And what a powerful prize: to turn consumers into investors, into co-creators.

7 Finance

In the progressive business of the 21st century, openness plays an incredibly important role in the finances of an organization. So important, in fact, that there is a whole chapter dedicated to that topic in Chapter Eight: Fair Finances.

8 Privacy

One note of caution: privacy must not be confused with openness or – worse – actually lost in this drive towards a more open world. It is true that notions of privacy are changing, particularly in younger people growing up having never known anything but a world with an internet. But, for some, that is an excuse to ride roughshod over people's reasonable expectations and rights to robust personal privacy.

So, as managers, employers and marketers, we must treat privacy with the highest regard. In general, people must have control over their own data and must not feel exposed without their consent and forewarning.

'Open and appropriately private' is the goal.

9 COMPETITION

Given all of this openness, where does competition fit? What *is* competition in the context of a more open, more connected 21st century? Who are we competing with? And why?

As my business partner and long-term collaborator Pete Burden commented as I published this extract on my blog 'Competition (as we have previously understood it) only makes sense in a world of scarcity and underlying a lot of what you are saying about openness is the opposite of scarcity – an abundance of easily replicated information and data'. He is right. And it is unresolved both in this book and in my mind.

It is true that notions of competition are changing. You must have noticed, as I have, the rise of the use of terms like 'frenemy' and 'co-opetition'. What is interesting is how digital culture is beginning to change organizational culture. On the internet, linking to other good content is what makes the web tick. Which led old-school business people to question 'why would we link to him, he works for the competition?' And on the internet, communities grow organically, messily, collaboratively and together create valuable ecosystems – and then the question from old-school (and logical) business is 'so who owns this?' which creates all kinds of brain-wrangling challenges for intellectual property law and for community members. Take Facebook, for example: is the value in the platform, or in the user base (i.e. the community)? And if it is indeed the community, what is their reward, their share scheme and payback?

Finally, on competition, it may seem that we are entering a world of abundance but one crucial constraint may be worthy of our attention. In the end, whilst we collaborate much more and work closely in co-opetition with traditional competitors, the available attention for what we provide may be scarce. Competition is not going away (for many, it is massively intensifying) – it is adapting and evolving in this more open world.

Summary

Openness is a fascinating topic and trend. Like a force of nature, it is awesomely powerful and not always benign or kind to those on the receiving end. And, like a force of nature, the huge power that it possesses can be partially harnessed. In business, our tendency is try to resist openness. Business usually wants closed-ness. It wants control, narrowness, monopoly, few rather than many, integration, quality, secrecy. Very often, business wants to be opaque. Generally, business people find the concept of organizational openness terrifying.

But, regardless, its power grows. Society is becoming more and more connected, which is leading to more and more openness. We can batten down the hatches, hate what it brings, and hope that it passes, and ideally soon. Or we can harness its energy, go with it, run full force with it and throw everything we have into being more open. In this chapter we have looked at ways to do so. To make it happen, as everything else in this book, will require grit and vision, and will lead to extremely positive cultural change.

As progressive business people, this is a wonderful opportunity and a force we can channel to help us make things better.

FURTHER READING

- *Wikinomics* – Don Tapscott and Anthony D. Williams
- *Open Leadership* – Charlene Li

CHAPTER SIX

CHANGE VELOCITY

In addition to organizational openness, another fundamental characteristic of organizations in this progressive movement is their ability to change very rapidly. And
their propensity to do so. For me it's one of their most
violent and disruptive advantages.

These fast-moving, fast-changing new players eat away
at industry incumbents' market share through their ability
to learn, iterate and change, loop after loop, many times
faster than the old guard.

Another change! Another change! Another change!
POW. Amazon vs. Barnes & Noble (US)/Waterstones
(UK), Netflix vs. Blockbuster, Threadless vs. GAP.

This is not just a business imperative – governments
and not-for-profits must also speed up. Google chairman,
Eric Schmidt, recently quoted Andy Grove, the long-
serving CEO of Intel, who said at a dinner back in 1995
'High tech runs three times faster than normal businesses.
And the government runs three times slower than normal
businesses. So we have a nine-times gap.' If government
would like to emulate the success and practices of Silicon
Valley, then they have a great deal of flexibility and speed
to find in themselves.

And related to this, one of their other great emerging
characteristics is their ability to U-turn. By U-turn I am

not just talking about product innovation, I'm talking about wholesale changes of direction.

Whatever you think of it, Facebook has been absolutely brilliant at doing something, hearing a load of feedback, and doing a public U-turn within hours or days. It doesn't always, and has returned to the same initiatives and goals over time, but generally Facebook and CEO Mark Zuckerberg have shown a remarkable willingness to adjust course or roll-back from controversial changes in the face of uproar and media backlash.

I thought of this characteristic again having followed the interesting story of Netflix, a US-based company that provides streaming media services and DVD rental.

If you haven't already heard, Netflix made some bold changes to their product, dividing the whole business in two with no consultation. They called the DVD mailing business Qwikster, and kept Netflix as the business focused solely on streaming.

There followed a sustained outcry, with reports of subscriber anger and a drop in share price. Then, 23 days later, they reversed the decision, as reported on paidContent.org: 'That Was Qwik: Netflix Dumps Qwikster, Won't Split DVD-Streaming Accounts'.

I always admire a U-turn:

1 You tried to innovate and make change – that takes guts and brainpower.
2 You listened – that takes ears!
3 You are humble enough to admit publicly that you were wrong – that takes guts.

Now, just before I began writing this, I was speaking with a team in a gigantic multinational bank. Some young talents in a development programme for top potential future stars are working on launching an innovative new business idea. Their biggest challenge is what they describe as the internal 'conservatism'. Making change in that organization is really, really hard. Scarily hard when you think about the above.

So what we are experiencing here is the ability of organizations to rapidly adapt to the world around them.

WHAT IS CHANGE VELOCITY?

A mate of mine called David has worked his whole career in sales. He is a proud salesman through and through. And he half-jokingly introduced me to one of his favourite concepts a few years ago: 'revenue velocity'. This is not how much work the client needs doing in total, but how quickly they need or want to invest that budget. At the time I found it a hilarious encapsulation of his deliberately cultivated salesman persona, both good and bad (though in time, running my own services business, I've learnt to appreciate the wisdom in it).

This phrase makes me think about an organization's change velocity – its ability to change quickly. Change velocity of an organization is its ability to change quickly. Not just with agility – the ability to shift focus rapidly – because an organization can be agile without internally changing. Not just with speed – the speed at which an organization moves – because again, an organization can move quickly without changing. And not just the ability to evolve – an organization can evolve effectively over time, but can it do so quickly enough?

The higher an organization's change velocity, the faster it can shift its focus, the faster it can execute, and the faster it can fundamentally change itself.

Why must 21st-century organizations be able to change so quickly?

In simple terms the argument is easy: because the world is changing so much more quickly. And specifically not the world elsewhere, over there in a distant corner of the globe, somehow removed and less relevant. Today, in the global marketplace, connected as we are by technology and systems, those far-off changes in 'the world elsewhere' mean that the external environment directly around our organizations is shifting rapidly, unexpectedly and disruptively. Most importantly, we have to get better at changing to handle the big shift from a world where we seek continuous growth to a world where we seek 'betterness', as Umair Haque would put it.

As a result of this compelling blend of drivers and trends we have to be conscious of, and work at, our ever-increasing our change velocity.

GLOBAL SHIFTS AND BLACK SWANS

It has become a cliché but, in a world of continuous disruption, change is the only constant.

Let's remind ourselves of some of the recent volatility and disruption in the global political and economic landscape:

- Lehman Brothers and the corresponding global financial system meltdown
- Double-dip recession 2007 to the present day
- The Arab Spring
- Rise of BRIC (Brazil, Russia, India, China) as new economic powerhouses – in particular the rise of China
- US stagnation
- Euro crisis, with Ireland, Greece, Portugal and Spain in various states of deep financial malaise
- Occupy movement
- Fukushima nuclear plant meltdown, Japan
- Wikileaks and *Guardian* campaigns against News Corporation
- The deaths of Bin Laden and Gaddafi

In his brilliant book, *Black Swan*, Nassim Nicholas Taleb described how organizations are geared up for expected risks – things that have happened before. These are 'white swans' – normal crises. But Taleb illustrates how the most cataclysmic, impactful, disorienting crises are entirely without precedent – we cannot prepare for them using scenarios, or simply adjust and prepare for what has happened before. These are 'black swans'. Unimaginable until they have been discovered, preposterous until they happen. Some of the above were black swans, while others were known possible outcomes. Combined, they represent a great deal of change.

In addition to these geopolitical and black-swan events, society too has evolved (or changed, at least!).

ACTIVISM AND CAMPAIGNING IN NETWORKS

In society, a new generation of activism has emerged. At the time of writing, in my home town of Brighton on the sunny south coast of England, a campaign has spread through the social networks connecting up people living in the city who are outraged at the alleged bullying of a breast-feeding mother in a local restaurant, with a number of fellow customers telling her 'she should be more discrete'. I first heard of it on Twitter, and quickly saw friends and friends of friends sharing the news, commenting on the original blog post (which currently has 100-odd comments) and then details of a planned 'flashmob' protest on Facebook. Facebook CEO Mark Zuckerberg has often talked of the platform as being a 'social utility' which 'removes friction from sharing'. The campaign ended up in the national and local press, on regional TV and was a brilliant success for a small group of busy (and probably tired!) mothers. Could a grassroots local campaign have spread as quickly with as little effort 50 years ago?

Clearly, this trend is not just about local campaigns. A new kind of campaigning organization is possible in the 21st century, take Occupy, of course, or The Tea Party in the US, or the Save The Forests campaign in the UK. These digitally networked, purpose-driven campaigns can quickly form and perform, seeming to emerge out of nowhere before applying very real influence on the issues of their choice.

And the result is that – as an organization on the wrong side of a campaign, rightly or wrongly – you can go from pootling along in business-as-usual mode, to facing a full-scale crisis, with your brand name trending on Twitter, connected activists overwhelming your website, and journalists combing through digital information – all in less than the time that it used to take to craft a press release.

TECHNOLOGY DISRUPTIONS

The influence of technology is woven throughout this book. We look at specifics, both further on in this chapter and Chapter Seven: Tech DNA. Suffice to say that the role of technology in driving the pace of change has been paramount – indeed, of more influence than any other individual cause.

NOBODY CHANGED THE RULES (YET)

It is also worth noting that one of the tensions that the 21st-century organization must deal with is that the rules of the game, and in particular the law, lag behind the present-day realities of our businesses.

The law must necessarily follow society – it cannot be designed in advance and put on the shelf, ready for when that unforeseen, black-swan event suddenly comes out of nowhere. So it is that the law follows events in the real world, and always has done.

However, some would say that we are in a period where there has been a wholesale paradigm shift, driven by technology and media, behind which the law is particularly lagging today. For businesses, that means the rules have not changed. Regulators and law courts still demand 20th century behaviour, which can provide a strong counter-pull to the necessity to evolve (we have also found in our work that it can provide a gold-plated excuse not to change – a crutch or a shield to hide behind).

In particular, the law around intellectual property feels distinctly 20th century. For example, copyright has been pretty binary – either you can remix my music or all rights are reserved and you cannot do anything with it (legally!). A brilliant project called Creative Commons has created a series of licences, which owners of intellectual property (usually the creators themselves) can use to provide more nuanced agreements to balance their desire for appropriate control with their desire to let other people benefit from their creations. So I can publish my music now under an Attribution-NonCommercial licence from Creative Commons, which means, in simple terms: 'you can do whatever you want with it as long as you attribute me and don't make money from whatever thing you go on to produce'. That's great, but what if I help Mr or Mrs Big Company come up with their new ground-breaking idea, but I submitted it to them via a marketing-friendly 'crowdsourcing' website? Or what if I spend ten hours a week solving problems for my local council – what's my deal? And how am I protected? And what is fair?

It will be fascinating to see how the law changes to fit an age of changed notions and expectations around sharing, ownership, creation and collaboration, which will affect all businesses.

THE BIGGEST REASON WE NEED TO GET BETTER AT CHANGING QUICKLY

However, there is a more fundamental reason why our businesses need to get better at responding to change, more than all of the above put together.

That is the perilous state of the environment.

If our businesses do not lead huge transformation in how modern life happens in the 21st century, we are all screwed. We have run out of time. The ice is melting, the seas are emptying of fish stocks, the weather systems are changing, the water is running out, many species are threatened or worse. We close our eyes and hum while the planet slips into an accelerating period of poor health. And, right now, most business feels like part of the problem rather than the solution.

We have to change the vested interests, the way things have always been done, the cultures and norms in every organization, every economy, every nation state. All of these require huge change in individuals and organizations and industries and government. The status quo is the biggest single threat to the future of humanity. Seriously.

So, as the challenges presented by all of these external factors come to life, society will begin to wake up and change will become the premium factor – a much desired and celebrated quality. Investors, employees, senior manag-

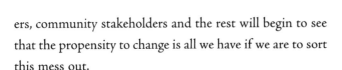

ers, community stakeholders and the rest will begin to see that the propensity to change is all we have if we are to sort this mess out.

For that reason alone, understanding and increasing the change velocity of our organizations is absolutely vital.

What are the benefits of improving our change velocity?

- Learning sooner, which leads to better decision-making including more effective use of resources.
- Staying closer to customer needs, which leads to better new product development, greater loyalty, greater market share and higher employee engagement.
- Greater resilience, which leads to a more stable organization, the attraction and retention of the best employees and customers and higher long-term results and returns.
- Continuing relevance in a volatile world, which leads to long-term contributions and sustenance to all stakeholders from employees and communities through to stockholders and economies.
- Lower risk, by 'following fast' and rapidly adapting to other organization's innovations (rather than always pioneering).
- All of which leads to competitive advantage – being the best, soonest, and therefore winning.
- Fundamentally contributing to the development of a sustainable global society.

So what areas influence an organization's change velocity?

We're going to break this down into four categories — each with its own subset of levers and buttons that can be pulled and pushed to speed up the organization's ability to change. Those categories are:

1 Personal factors
2 Organizational factors
3 Behaviours
4 Counter-forces

1 PERSONAL FACTORS

You may be wondering, what does the personal have to do with my organization's ability to change? The perspective of *Culture Shock* is that an organization is made up of people, rather than of bricks, or inventory, or processes. People *are* the organization. In order to improve the way a whole organization responds to change, we must transform the way in which the many individuals that make up that organization each respond to change.

It is well understood that it is normal to find change difficult. Just check out the shelves of the self-help sections in a book shop or do a quick Google for 'behaviour change'. So, given that change is difficult, if we are to help change our organizations personally, and credibly lead such change, we must ourselves understand change intimately and be evolving ourselves.

ATTITUDE

The highest order lever, then, is our own attitude and approach towards change. We must develop a personal

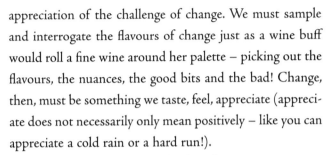

appreciation of the challenge of change. We must sample and interrogate the flavours of change just as a wine buff would roll a fine wine around her palette – picking out the flavours, the nuances, the good bits and the bad! Change, then, must be something we taste, feel, appreciate (appreciate does not necessarily only mean positively – like you can appreciate a cold rain or a hard run!).

We must take the attitude that change is a constant, and that what we can influence is the way we respond to it and flex with and around it.

And we must respect, appreciate and learn constantly about what it is like to change personally, developing over time a strong understanding of how we personally respond to change.

Understanding things like:

- What do I personally find hard to change in myself?
- How do I typically respond to change at first?
- What motivators really work for me to see change through?

In short, our attitude must be two-fold: embracing of change, and respectful of the consequences and demands of change. Doing so gets us ready for everything that follows.

HABITS

My limited understanding of the power of habits has been gained from two brilliant professors of behaviour change – Ben Fletcher and Karen Pine. In their Do Something Different programme, they have developed a guide to personal change based on their academically robust research, which is now being used on a large scale in deprived areas in the UK, to enable individuals to loosen the personal habits that prevent change.

As I have learnt from Ben and Karen, our habits are a complex web of behaviours that may control us more than we realize. And these habits are fairly hard to wiggle out of – they interlink and hold one another in place. We are, to quite a large degree, 'habit machines' – much less conscious of our decision making than we at first realize.

Think about this:

- When you take a shower, in which order do you wash yourself?
- How do you travel to work each day?
- Where do you normally sit on a bus or a train?
- Do your arguments with loved ones tend to have particular patterns? If so, what are the patterns?
- What do you choose for lunch and where do you go?

This mesh of habits both helps by making the nuts and bolts of everyday life simpler, and hinders by providing a barrier to us changing the habits we wish to. So, if we shift the context to that of you at work, you may start to find habits there: how you respond to communications, both physical and digital; how you react under pressure; how you give and receive praise; how you say yes and say no and who to. Can you think of habits you have at work? Can you observe habits and patterns in those you work with?

The Do Something Different programme operates on the basis that loosening up the grip of some of our most basic, 'unimportant' habits makes way for us to be able to take more transformative personal steps.

So if the purpose of you reading this book is to change how business happens in the 21st century, and we agree that organizations are made up of individuals, then one of the keys to change is going to be the individual changing of habits: starting with your own!

LISTENING

In order to be able to make personal changes, and therefore to become part of the positively evolving future organization, like Johnny Five in *Short Circuit*, you 'neeeeeed input'.

This skill is in managing your attention, especially in listening, in dialogue and in empathy.

The successful leader in change senses and pays attention to what the market is doing, to what customers are saying (and not saying), to what their colleagues are feeling and seeing themselves. (I'm guessing that as a reader of this kind of book you already know that.)

This is why the business press has notably shifted in the past five years to a focus on things like Emotional Quotient (EQ) over IQ, to celebrating right-brained qualities like creativity and empathy over linearity and number crunching.

In my first and only proper job a very experienced and quirky sales person told me that we have two ears and one mouth and, in sales, one should use them in that ratio — it's an old saw, of course, and one you've no doubt heard yourself many times. I suggest, as so many others have before, that the same applies to anyone who desires to create change through working with people. If we are to lead change (not just once, but continuously) it would be better to listen twice as much as talk.

HUMILITY

Finally, in order to accelerate our own change velocity – which frankly sounds like something out of a bad science fiction novel – we have to cultivate our own humility.

It is one thing to hear feedback that tells us that something we have done, or are responsible for, must change. It is another to act on that feedback and accept that we were wrong. Yet this is the very quality we need to wash through our teams, our organizations and our business community – a willingness to be wrong, an acceptance of other people's opinions and ideas, the self-belief and humility to publicly change course. Because this is the fuel of change velocity.

We cannot change by getting it right every time. We cannot go from stasis to 'perfect next step'! We have to make a mess, learn-by-doing, and crack on without losing vital time in endless paralyzing focus groups and internal discussions.

To change, we have to *do*. And to do the big things that need doing (like changing how our whole organization behaves, one step at a time) we need humility and self-awareness.

By cultivating humility and demonstrating failure, and by rapidly gathering up the self-awareness and learning that come with failure, we open up new possibilities around change and flexibility that are simply not available otherwise. We welcome in unexpected consequences, put up less resistance and move faster in response to black swans, we learn and change more constantly. None of which is possible if our posture is that 'I'm already perfect'.

2 ORGANIZATIONAL FACTORS

Now having explored some of the personal factors, let's look at the organizational traits and areas where change velocity can be driven from and what that can achieve.

AGILITY

I was speaking at a conference recently. The panellist on just before me was from a national train company, working in PR. He described the challenges they have in today's connected world when there is a crisis in their rail operation (for example if a train gets derailed).

He said, 'ten years ago we had two hours to get a handle on what had happened and prepare to brief the media, five years ago with the mainstream adoption of the mobile phone that dropped to twenty minutes, now – with smartphones, picture messaging, Twitter and Facebook – we have twenty seconds before the world knows more about the crisis than we do'.

This is what is demanded of our organizations today. Pow! Something happens. Twenty seconds later, the world knows about it. A plane crash-landing in the Hudson river, the king of pop Michael Jackson dying, a politician being arrested or an oil company facing an oil spill. You and your team have a buffer of twenty seconds between something happening and it being potentially shared globally and with no friction or cost.

We call this realtime. It means that the lag between what happens and the world knowing about it is ever-closer to realtime – they are nearly the very same. The buffer is all but gone.

We have already looked at the accelerative role played by online platforms – not just in the external media, as in this train company and Twitter example, but also in the way employees generate feedback for managers in HCL, in how customers innovate continuously for T-shirt company Threadless and for other businesses through the crowdsourcing of Innocentive. The phenomenon of realtime isn't just a media and external communications thing: the need to be more agile and connected is a whole business thing.

THE OODA MODEL

When John Boyd, the American ex-fighter pilot, developed his OODA model, I wonder whether he saw how broad its use might eventually become. Originally conceived to describe how combat happens between fast jets, the OODA model illustrates that decision making happens in loops – we make a decision, see what impact that has, make another decision, see what impact that then has and so on. Here's what OODA stands for:

- Observe – what is going on in the environment around me?
- Orient – what is my place in that environment, where am I in relation to everything else?
- Decide – given all of that, what shall I do as my next step?
- Act – implementing the decision

And repeat. So, one thing to like about OODA is its iterative nature. That alone suits the organizational environment that we are exploring here, where change is constant. But the big takeaway from the OODA model is not that decisions are in chains, linked together, all part of a constant process of decision-making. The big takeaway of the model is actually that the faster you can go through the OODA loop, the more likely you are to win.

Hold on a sec, you say. Perhaps fast decision making isn't the only thing that leads to winning in business or in combat or in policy-making! Maybe the best decision wins, and we should emphasize putting time and thought into patiently crafting the best decision? That may be true. For me, though, the shift to thinking in the OODA mode is that we are no longer seeking 'the single best decision for all time' – we are instead freed up to make a whole series of 'the best decision right now' choices. As a result, the stakes are actually lowered. In the OODA mode we are shifted from thinking mode into doing mode, and we move from planning and considering into actively learning more about what works and what doesn't. To me, intuitively, this is absolutely right for a world of volatility and ever-present change.

READY, FIRE, AIM: AGILE DEVELOPMENT; AND ALWAYS IN BETA

Other people, like the brilliantly challenging management thinker Tom Peters, have characterized and long promoted this same shift in decision making from 'Ready, Aim, Fire!' to 'Ready, Fire!, Aim'. And, in software development and in entrepreneurial start-ups (of any kind), this emphasis has been gaining momentum steadily.

A start-up founder knows that the speed her team can move at is one of her few advantages against the big players, and knows that – with a limited pile of cash (or indeed no cash at all) – the best thing she can do is drive her business to move more quickly.

Similarly, an experienced software engineer knows that the lowest-risk approach to hitting his deadline and shipping some high-quality code may not be by working to a carefully developed and endlessly detailed plan, but instead by breaking down the whole project into a series of 'sprints', chunking the whole development into much smaller batches, and then re-prioritizing the next steps every two weeks. This Agile approach to software development has gained in momentum over the past decade and, at its very core, is the philosophy that things *will and always do* change during the project – both in the environment and in the learning of the development team and the client – and that harnessing that change is the key to success. There is nothing more demoralizing than following a 12-month plan that is already out of date in week three: Agile software development recognizes this and flips traditional linear approaches to project management on their head.

The good news is that Agile as a project management approach has been leaking out of its homeland of software development into many other organizational silos, and into government too. Project owners, managers and teams are voting with their feet – an agile approach makes sense in the 21st century.

So what happens when we take these increasingly trendy approaches into business? We shift from 'perfectly planned' to 'always learning' or perhaps 'Beta'. Beta is another term borrowed from the world of software development – the Alpha version is the shaky first prototype of a new web service or technology, the Beta version the next iteration with some of the most obvious glitches fixed – still incomplete but ready to share with a wider group of people for testing in the real world.

Being in Beta has since become as much an attitude as a formal state: Google's Gmail was in Beta for years and had millions of daily active users! Since late 2009 the financial mobile payment startup Square has signed up one million retailers by offering an innovative mobile approach to handling financial payments that has entirely caught traditional financial services providers off guard. I'm sure that Square changes every day, if not every week. Always in Beta has become a slogan for an OODA-like attitude that says 'this web app/restaurant/teaching curriculum is never going to be complete – it will always be tweaked, improved and iterated'.

3 BEHAVIOURS

If our businesses are going to move with the cat-like agility described above, what will underpin that? What new behaviours must emerge? Which existing behaviours must change or die?

COLLABORATING

First, it seems fairly obvious to say, but it will be impossible to move at the requisite new-speed-of-business if the people in our teams and across our departments are unable to collaborate.

When the train crisis happens, if there are now only 20 seconds instead of the two hours available ten years ago, then our man at the train company cannot afford any internal friction. On behalf of the company, he simply cannot tolerate politicking, unnecessary bureaucracy, or delay. He needs a network of highly responsive, empowered and helpful colleagues to move at realtime speed.

Silos do not support this kind of collaboration. In fact, they are diametrically opposed to enabling this kind of collaboration. Yet so many people describe the silos and silo behaviour in their organizations.

Where does silo thinking come from and who can change it? Leaders must address these issues, and especially their own personal behaviour that contributes to this.

Leaders at all levels must model collaboration, must reward collaboration and unlock the blockers of collaboration.

FAILING

Second, as we have previously explored in both Chapter Three: Progressive People and Chapter Four: Conscious Leadership, shifting organizational perceptions of failure is incredibly important in the organization of the 21st century.

A lack of understanding and celebrating of failure leads to butt-covering, which in turn (without wanting to sound like Yoda) leads to a clogging of the pipes of collaboration. Failure itself may not be the greatest cost in an organization but, instead, the *fear* of failure which actually paralyzes decision making and creates enormous stress for the people in the organization.

Greater willingness to fail will lead to greater levels of trust between people in the organization and a higher degree of honesty throughout. Indeed, if we see failing as learning, then the opportunity to fail more can create organizations that genuinely cherish and work towards learning and our companies will truly become 'learning organizations' which restlessly adapt and move forwards.

REWARDING

Third, what your organization fundamentally rewards hugely affects its change velocity. For clarity, when I say 'what your organization rewards', I mean what it *really* rewards – not just what it says it values. We've all been in organizations where there is an espoused value of integrity, only to see behaviour that is quite the opposite, or where thinking differently is internally branded as a core value, yet the people in the organization actually squash new ideas and prefer to rinse and repeat, sticking with the 'way things have always been done'.

So, to accelerate their change velocity, organizations must truly reward the bundle of behaviours that unlock flexibility and agility: behaviours like personal development, business change, creativity and innovation, risk-taking and failure, and collaboration.

The organizations that do reward these qualities do so with both hard and soft rewards: in pay packets, bonuses, promotions and so on, and in 'softer' but perhaps even more impactful ways such as prizes, public visibility internally and externally, in one-on-ones and through coaching. And this will influence literally everyone in the organization: from a founder or CEO to the receptionist or groundskeeper.

This truly nourishes an organization striving to operate faster and better. A groundswell of collaboration and energy for change from the people in the whole team, in the whole organization, pushing for a better organization that can dance like a butterfly and sting like a bee. What is rewarded is absolutely key.

4 COUNTERFORCES

As we hurtle into this realtime world, where a friend uploads a photo of their meal in a fine restaurant to their chosen social network seconds before they devour it and then leaves an online review of the food before they've paid their bill, where organizations are monitoring and acting on feedback continuously gathered through forums and review sites, it is worth recognizing that there are the beginnings of a counter-revolution or at least obvious counter-forces against this always-on way of life. And rightly so.

For the constant on-ness of a realtime world cannot be healthy. Some researchers talk about the side-effects of 'continuous partial attention', the state where we humans are continuously monitoring a variety of information sources but with a thin 'partial' slice of our attention. Is it healthy to be plugged in to our mobile phone, our email, news headlines, an internal collaboration tool, one or two or three social networks *and* have conversations with loved ones and colleagues? What is this doing to our relationships, our brains, our blood pressure? What is it like for a child to grow up in a world where its parents are often absorbed by a little black rectangle they hold in their hands, expression frowning in concentration, thumb scrolling away? When do we start talking seriously about internet addiction?

Other researchers celebrate instead the virtues of 'flow': that dream-like state where everything comes together without any fuss, where you are 'in the zone', uninterrupted, locked in, all of your attention poured onto one single area of focus. And – in the flow state – the report practically writes itself, the spreadsheet starts to add up, the bookshelf gets categorized, the garden looks good again. Where is the flow in a realtime world? How can an organization achieve greatness when its people are spreading their attention so thinly every day?

Artists and thinkers are also playing with notions of slowness, fighting back against the incessant speed of modern life. Jeff Bezos, CEO of Amazon, has funded a brilliant project that has built 'The 10,000 year clock' in a remote Texan hillside. The clock chimes once a year, is designed to function for 10,000 years, and every single chime will be unique from any before or after. In a disposable, short-term world, this project is designed to strive for a longevity that has become lost in the hurly-burly and speed of the 21st century. And, of course, there is the Slow Food Movement, celebrating the virtues of patience, time, space, peace.

Lastly, a debate continues about whether change is even accelerating at all. Some people say that of course it is, and point to all of the things we discuss in this book and more. In fact, futurist Ray Kurzweil believes that we are only at the earliest part of an accelerating phase that will get substantially faster over the next 50 years. He argues that, as technology develops, so it has a compound effect on each wave of progress and so further accelerates until we reach 'The Singularity' where human and computer intelligence are merged but that's a whole 'nother book! The anti-speeding-up lobby resists, and points to the fact that our grandparents generation went from the horse and cart and steam-powered trains to men on the moon, smart phones with inconceivable computing power and kids playing and learning in online virtual worlds. Fair point.

The point is this: the world is changing. And to many people, it feels like change is accelerating. Whatever the case, it is certainly true that the majority of our businesses, organizations and institutions are unable to move quickly enough to keep up any more. They are increasingly out of touch. What we have to do is increase the velocity that they are able to change at, in order that they remain relevant and bring their resources to bear on the problems that need solving.

How can you speed up your organization's change velocity?

Here are eight areas from which you can positively influence your organization's willingness and ability to change and change quickly. It's a dry looking list, but trust me – the contents, if applied, are electric.

1 Planning
2 Structures
3 Processes
4 Systems
5 Attitudes
6 Hiring and firing
7 Rewards
8 Personal change

1 Planning

Activity in brief

Start planning in six-month cycles. And plan in as high a contingency budget as you reasonably can to jump on unexpected opportunities or emergencies that arise. That's it.

Description

Most plans resist change. Or at least bad plans do. Although the world understandably craves control – people like to know what's going to happen – progressive businesses need and take more flexible approaches to planning.

If you see the same world that I do, how on *earth* can we reasonably do a five-year plan?

To improve your change velocity, you need to bring the planning horizon right back into the present day, back from those misty forecasted mountains out there in five years' time; of exceptional, uninterrupted, white-swans-only business-as-usual. And with your opportunity/contingency budget, you can start to be more responsive to what happens along the way.

Sure, there'll be resistance (and perhaps death threats) from others in your organization – no matter how big or small. Maybe you'll need to play the game a little bit, and fill in their long-term planning spread-sheets. But you can start planning in a more adaptive, agile way. It will spread (slowly) unless you're a very senior manager, in which case 'hey, get on with it!'

2 Structures

Activity in brief
Start creating and encouraging small, inter-departmental, cross-functional teams around projects and initiatives. Start doing what you would otherwise do alone or in a small group but, instead, in more mixed groups – bringing in 'outsiders'.

Description
Deliberately include people from parts of the organization which your part usually competes with. And, if you have the chance, invite the mavericks – the upcoming ambitious talents who know their way around and want to get stuff done. Set a peer-to-peer, collaborative tone in these groups, and allow the group to prove the power of collaboration over time. Keep bureaucracy to a minimum, and where possible keep things low-key and under the radar.

Remember Gore's lattice structure in Chapter Three: Progressive People? These small inter-departmental teams will massively improve connectivity in your organization. They will build an important network of alliances that can be called on in crises.

Through our own consulting work we have found, to our surprise, that such groups can be seen as subversive – a clear sign that the organization is badly silo'd and needs exactly this kind of approach to collaboration.

3 Processes

Activity in brief
Do a quick audit of the processes you have which mean that it takes you hours, days or weeks to respond to something that you need to be able to respond to in minutes (think of the train guy and his '20 seconds to prepare and respond').

Description
Reflect on what's blocking this in your organization. Where do the problems with responding quickly lie? How serious are they? What can you do about them? What are the costs (current or potential) of the delays caused by this bureaucracy?

Now put this in a short document, which clearly and accurately describes the costs and potential worst-case scenarios and get the processes changed.

If you are a senior manager or CEO in a large organization start encouraging your people to identify and flag up ways in which the organization is constraining their ability to respond quickly. You could also consider the approach that Indian systems integrator, HCL, takes by allowing any employee to hold support functions like finance, HR, admin and senior management to account by raising a 'ticket' from the employee to the department in question, underpinned with a strict and transparent commitment to reply within certain parameters.

4 Systems

Activity in brief
Get some Buzz monitoring set up, or – if it already is elsewhere in the organization – get access to the relevant reports. Then feed the snippets and insights you get into your teams, your colleagues and obviously into your own planning, thinking and doing. Congratulations, you are now moving at close to realtime!

Description
Buzz monitoring is technology that automatically scours the web for mentions of keywords of your choice. It is a way for you to get closer to realtime by staying more up to date with what's happening in the outside world. Appropriate keywords might be your brand name, the product or services names that you are responsible for, your competitors brands or your customers names – it depends on whatever it is that you need to be on top of.

A very simple but excellent place to start is Google Alerts. You can set up a Google Alert in seconds, and then Google will email you 'mentions' of those keywords either 'as it happens', daily or weekly (I recommend daily for a good balance between being overwhelmed and being out of date by the time you get them.)

At the higher end, offering more sophisticated filtering and reporting, are buzz monitoring technologies like those provided by my personal buddies at Brandwatch and a host of others. If you work in a corporation, someone somewhere will almost certainly have subscribed to one of these providers – find out who!

5 Attitudes

Activity in brief

Nurture more agile approaches to getting stuff done. Send a motivated project manager (or go yourself) on an Agile Project Management course. Start using agile to manage your projects.

Description

Spread awareness and excitement around you about the 'Always in Beta' approach to launching new things – it doesn't matter if it's a new expenses process or a glossy new piece of marketing material.

Celebrate failure. Talk about your own failures, don't hide them. If you have one, tell your boss that you believe the organization needs to be more supportive of failure and that you're going to start talking about failure more. Encourage and reward failures in your own team. If you're brave enough, do a Church of Fail! (see Chapter Three: Progressive People).

6 Hiring & Firing

Activity in brief
Be more rigorous about who is right for the organization and the journey it's going on – to get that right, you have to raise the standards on who gets hired and – necessarily – who gets fired.

Description
Simple, but will take time to have an effect, as hiring and firing generally don't happen overnight, but essentially what you are trying to do here is increase the blend of people you have in your organization who are change-friendly. So hire people that appear to – and can evidence – their ability to flex and their welcoming of change and evolution. These people will be more likely to be able to demonstrate self-awareness of their habits and perhaps of habits they have changed. They will be energized and excited about change, possibility, challenge.

The other practical reality is that, to make this work, you and your organization will need to move people on that absolutely refuse to and bitterly resist change. It is not good for them to be in an organization that is pushing to adapt and move quickly, and it is definitely not good for everyone else that is trying to do so. The word 'firing' here, in this book, might seem out of place. A little harsh, a little old school, a little flippant maybe. But, as my friend Will Morey puts it, this is incredibly important: 'Breaking up is hard to do. Get better at it. Learning how to let people move on from the organization is critical.'

If the future of your organization depends on its ability to change (which it does, basically) then hiring and firing are absolutely crucial in getting the best possible group of people in the organization to adjust to whatever the future throws at them, both in the moment and in market changes that happen over time.

7 Rewards

Activity in brief
Make changing and evolving a part of everyone's job, and hugely reward those efforts to change.

Description
Build into your own role description, and those of the people in your team or wider organization, clear responsibilities about changing and evolving the

organization. What gets managed, gets done and, by explicitly making elements of change velocity part of peoples jobs, you vastly improve the likelihood of it actually happening. So, incentives and rewards are powerful allies in helping shift your team, your division or your start-up group towards this culture of 'we embrace change'.

Ensure that you ask any reports to include examples of positive change that they have made both in the organization and in themselves in their annual reviews, and be sure to reward them for doing so – both in financial and non-financial ways. (In our team we have a shield of win that peers pass from one to another to celebrate success – the point is that it isn't only about job descriptions, you can have fun with it.)

8 Personal change

Activity in brief

Those endlessly challenging words from Gandhi: 'You must be the change you wish to see in the world'.

Description

To really make this happen you will have to speed up your own personal change velocity. To embrace change personally, to role model the personal development necessary to overcome the habits and behaviours that resist change, to dance in the moment when crises or unexpected events happen, to roll with it, to accept and then celebrate failure in yourself and in others and the learning that it brings. Simple really, yes? No! Terribly difficult, and incredibly rewarding. No matter what level you operate at, you must lead in this. You must be the change you wish to see.

SUMMARY

In a world where change is constant, and possibly accelerating, our businesses will thrive or decay according to how quickly they can adapt. The media and communication environment in which we all now exist and participate is close to realtime: things happen, everybody knows about it, with a 20 second lag (and falling).

To thrive, to reach for our Purpose of Significance, and make a difference to the world, we have to increase our change velocity. As a side effect, we gain huge advantages – we move faster and better than others and so gain rewards; we individually become more flexible, more open and less resistant to the world around us and so gain rewards. Let's move. Now!

Next, appropriately given its role in Change Velocity and Organizational Openness, we will look at how the most progressive organizations actively nurture and develop a Tech DNA.

CHAPTER SEVEN

TECH DNA

Yesterday my two boys sat at the kitchen table, one playing a game on a laptop, the other clutching my wife's iPhone. They laughed, played together and apart, solved problems, stared into screens, toyed with technology. I don't think they know what technology is yet. For them it is just part of life – stuff that has always been there. And despite any guilt we may have about what is right and healthy for our children, the world that we live in today is populated with technology.

The world we live in is vastly different to that which we grew up in, thanks to technology. Big changes have occurred. And the changes continue at pace. As we touched on earlier, some of the most influential technology thinkers of this generation believe that, if anything, change is accelerating; that we have barely seen the start of it yet! Can you imagine a world more radically altered by technology, shifted exponentially further?

Listen to what renowned futurist and entrepreneur Ray Kurzweil has to say in his book *The Singularity Is Near*: 'By the end of this century, the non-biological portion of our intelligence will be trillions of trillions of times more powerful than unaided human intelligence.' He sees a world where our human intelligence is augmented by computing intelligence.

'Ridiculous!' you shout. But are we not already on that path?

Consider this, for example: in her book *Reality is Broken*, author Jane McGonigal writes that 'collectively, gamers have spent six million years playing the online multiplayer game World of Warcraft – about as long as Homo sapiens have been walking planet Earth. By that measure, we've spent as much time playing World of Warcraft as we've spent evolving as a species.' Can we underestimate the impact that technology is already having on our behaviour?

Technology is changing who we are, what we do and how we do it. In the context of this book, technology is a positive thing. We have looked already in chapters past at how the pioneers of 21st-century business already harness the power of technology to help them deliver smarter, more effective and – perhaps perversely – more human businesses.

And so, although technology is as woven through this book as it is through our lives, this chapter gathers together key principles and opportunities for you and your organization.

Where are our businesses today when it comes to technology?

The situation varies from organization to organization. But in general, technology has spent too long occupying either the blockading role of 'IT as police' or, worse, in the crushingly disappointing role of 'overhyped promises, and now nobody can use it'.

And to be clear here, we are not talking about high-tech as core business. We are not talking about R&D, and the development of technology to sell on. We are talking about digital innovation around the creation and delivery of their business, whether it be groceries, shoes or silicon chips.

So the questions for you are:

- To what extent does technology enable your organization to really fly?
- What is the average level of tech savviness in your team and the people directly around you?
- If you had to sum up your people's attitudes towards using technology to improve what you currently offer to the world, what would that one sentence be?
- How many non-technical geeks do you know of in the organization – people that *love* technology but do not occupy tech roles?
- What's the big potential tech shift that is out there for your organization that people/you are resisting?
- If you were to take one small step towards that big shift, what would it be?

Hold those thoughts, and let's take a look at some of the benefits available to pioneering organizations that make the most of technology without ending up in that predictable slump of over-promised, under-utilized technology #fail.

CREATING TECH DNA

In our consultancy work we see some clients diving straight in with brave, untested digital strategies, while others wait for their whole market to move before dipping a toe in. After a while I started asking myself 'do some organizations thrive because they are willing to embrace technology, or do they thrive because they are willing to innovate and be flexible and so take advantage of technology opportunistically?' Put another way, are the pioneering businesses taking a tech-centric approach, or a broader 'innovate and adopt change of any flavour' approach?

I don't have the answer, although I imagine it is more likely to be the latter.

Either way, the fact is that from my viewpoint the most successful organizations increasingly seem to be those which have an embracing attitude towards the disruption and opportunity that technology creates. Indeed, in many cases, it is part of their DNA.

So what is it like when an organization has technology in its DNA?

When an organization has technology in its DNA it:

- Typically moves before its peers to experiment with technology.
- Typically expects technology thinking to happen outside of just the IT or Technology areas – it expects marketers, R&D people, customer services, operations, retail and everyone else to be thinking 'how can technology help us improve this given area?'
- Usually takes an Agile/Beta approach to technology innovation and manages expectations accordingly.

- And so typically will opt for lightweight technology today rather than a turn-key solution in 12 months' time.
- Always puts the human aspect of how the technology will actually be used and valued over the whizz-bang feature set – prioritizing user-centred thinking and involvement over tech-for-tech's sake.

How does your organization do on such a checklist? Would you say your organization has Tech DNA? Are there people, areas or divisions that do and some that do not? What are the enablers where it is and what are the blockers where it is not?

WHY DOES A PROGRESSIVE BUSINESS NURTURE ITS TECH DNA?

The benefits of being a more digital, tech-savvy enterprise are fairly straightforward and, in today's day and age, also fairly meaty in terms of their payback:

- Learns more quickly, and so gains advantage and ROI sooner than others.
- Lowers risk by addressing IT and technology as ongoing part of business-as-usual rather than as big one-off 'game-changing' projects.
- Opens up previously unidentified new opportunities to meet its Purpose of Significance.
- Lowers risk and massively increases ROI by involving people all the way through any technology initiative.

Being cautious about dismissing the non-'natives'

Let me add a cautionary note on thinking that positive attitudes towards technology and especially digital relate only to age: we should exercise care when drawing over-simplistic conclusions about digital immigrants and digital natives, and the idea that the generations are completely apart when it comes to technology. I like the way the influential Berkman Center for Internet and Society at Harvard University puts it: 'Digital natives share a common global culture that is defined not by age, strictly, but by certain attributes and experiences in part defined by their experience growing up immersed in digital technology, and the impact of this upon how they interact with information technologies, information itself, one another, and other people and institutions. Those who were not "born digital" can be just as connected, if not more so, than their younger counterparts. And not everyone born since, say, 1982, happens to be a digital native.'

Oh, and if you let yourself off the hook with this 'I'm not a digital native like them younglings' rubbish, then it is time to step up – be a silver surfer instead:)

Unpicking definitions: what are Enterprise 2.0 and the Social business?

There is a lot of talk in business about both Enterprise 2.0 and, increasingly, about social business. Given that we are discussing technology in progressive organizations here, and that these two definitions (or buzzwords, depending on your perspective) are concerned with how organizations gain advantage by harnessing technology, it is probably worth taking a brief look into each 'definition' so that you can get down with the lingo!

In simple terms, Enterprise 2.0 is the IT community framing the internal support services and technologies they provide in the context of Web 2.0. That means technology approaches and systems that are:

■ More bottom-up or P2P than top-down in their architecture and behaviour.
■ More oriented towards the development of online communities around issues than the provision of information and services alone.

The important thing with Enterprise 2.0 is that it is very internally focused. In a utopian future (or a software vendor's marketing material) the dream is that your tumbleweed-y intranet of yesteryear, that people only used to download the expenses form and find out how much holiday they had left, is now this fuzzy, warm online community platform where knowledge sharing is happening, where new connections are being forged across the business, where good stuff happens 24/7/365.

Social business is similar to Enterprise 2.0 – they overlap substantially – but social business has emerged not just from IT but also from operations, marketing, brand and elsewhere. Social business is also a newer term, and so some of the definitions and practices are still emerging.

Social business tends to consider technology approaches and systems that:

■ Are both internal and external – beyond internal systems into the outside world too and the realm of dialogue and engagement with customers and other groups.
■ Go to the core of the organization – not just in enabling and supporting, but in how products and services are developed (e.g. crowdsourcing), in how people are hired and developed, how customer relationships are fostered and so on.

An important note also, for your dinner party conversations about the subtleties of Enterprise 2.0, social business and the like, is that there is a rival definition for social business that was coined by Muhammad Yunus, the founder of Grameen, who we looked at in Chapter One: Purpose and Meaning. For Yunus, a social business has absolutely nothing to do with technology per se:

'Social business is a cause-driven business. In a social business, the investors/owners can gradually recoup the money invested, but cannot take any dividend beyond that point. Purpose of the investment is purely to achieve one or more social objectives through the operation of the company, no personal gain is desired by the investors.'

In an ideal world we would honour Yunus' definition and find some new words to hang this stuff on. He is a great person making a brilliant difference in the world, and the world needs more businesses just as he describes. Unfortunately though, both definitions have momentum, and so in this book our definition is the former – not the Yunus version.

By the way, for me, this whole book is about social business. So although you might find that the social business community talk more about technologies, at Nixon-McInnes we believe that social business is about people first, and we hold Yunus' definition in mind too when we think about how businesses should behave – so everything in this book, for us, creates an awesome, unstoppable social business.

WHAT DO ENTERPRISE 2.0 AND SOCIAL BUSINESS HAVE IN COMMON?

Guess what? Both definitions have at their heart democracy, openness and change, all topics we've devoted whole chapters to.

These two technology mindsets or definitions are all about empowering people, about opening up boundaries and resources and creating transparency and porosity, and they are about realtime communication and flow. So everything we have worked through in this book, when applied to the technology infrastructure of organizations, is what those two definitions aspire to.

PEOPLE, UNLOCKED!

So what does a progressive business practically do with technology?

The four areas for you to drill into are as follows:

1 Flow tools
2 Collaboration platforms
3 Customer communities
4 Role of IT

1 FLOW TOOLS

From a digital communications perspective, we are moving towards a 'flow' paradigm.

To understand that, let's first backtrack a little. In the previous paradigm there was a kind of 'inbox/send and receive' paradigm – so in email I would send you an email and at some point you would reply, and so it would continue. Our inbox contained the communications we had to deal with, and it would fill up and empty and to begin with, this was manageable – content was reasonably finite in the early days. Eventually we began to get a lot of email. If we got into trouble, we might read *Getting Things Done* by David Allen or download a clever app – some kind of widely evangelized productivity religious system would rescue us!

Eventually, as you know, this became unsustainable. The exponential explosion of content and communications soon meant we could not keep up – whether that was with email, status updates on social networks, clips of cute kittens doing silly things on YouTube or inspiring videos of people doing TED-like talks. The metaphorical inbox overfloweth. And then some!

At some point, we had to give up on managing every piece of content. It got too much. Around the same time, Twitter really started to grow. And people with their heads still in the 'send and receive' paradigm asked questions like 'how do you stay up to date with Twitter?' A fair question from that point of view, but one that illustrates just how much has changed.

Facing that same question, *New York Times* journalist David Carr elegantly described it like this: 'At first, Twitter can be overwhelming, but think of it as a river of data rushing past that I dip a cup into every once in a while.' That is how flow tools work.

And that river analogy is really how many of us see the digital future unravelling: more 'flowy' than 'inboxy'. The web anthropologist and futurist Stowe Boyd has been influential in my awareness and ideas around this area, and it may have been from Stowe that I first heard the description of 'flow tools' (although I believe he may have moved on to 'liquid' in more recent times).

SO WHAT ARE FLOW TOOLS?

Flow tools are technologies or platforms that put an 'activity stream' of updates and conversations at their core. They use this model rather than the inbox approach, and allow

low-friction conversations and snippety updates to happen
throughout the course of the working week.

When they are functioning well, they lead to serendipi-
tous connections happening by forming a kind of 'ambient
awareness' amongst team members of what else is going on.

Here are some examples:

- Twitter – first and foremost
- Facebook – the status/activity stream part of the social
  network
- Yammer – a 'private Twitter' often used inside organizations to provide Twitter-like status updates
- Chatter – same again, from Salesforce.com, but links
  into CRM and other Salesforce resources

How can this help? Consider how Cristóbal Conde,
president and CEO of SunGard, described in an interview
with the *New York Times* how he is now able to distribute
vital client insights following meetings with senior customers: 'I'm not going to send that out in a broadcast voicemail to
every employee. But I can write five lines on Yammer, which
is about all it takes. A free flow of information is an incredible tool.' Precious information pumped into the bloodstream
of the organization, with very little effort and friction.

So, progressive businesses use flow tools to keep people
in the organization connected and moving at the speed of
events out there in the real world. Definitely a great lo-fi
way to speed up your organization's change velocity and
increase openness and empowerment. If in doubt, start

with Yammer. If in doubt, find a way to do it rather than waiting endlessly for the official go-ahead from IT.

2 COLLABORATION PLATFORMS

To separate these from flow tools is tricky as there is substantial overlap here due to the very blurry edges between emerging categories of technology. But here we need to look at some of the technologies and platforms that enable social businesses not only to share, but also to store knowledge and enable collaboration.

However, for the purpose of this book, we will determine that the main difference is that collaboration platforms meet a need posed by the main downside of flow tools: that good content can be lost in the flow and not stored somehow. I think of collaboration tools as better suited to holding good content to make it accessible in the future.

In particular, wikis represent everything Culture Shock is about in a technology. If you haven't used a wiki yet, you need to – either now or by the end of the day – go and edit and add something helpful to a page on Wikipedia. DO IT. (If you have, I apologize for patronizing you.)

A wiki is basically an editable web page – and one that is usually editable directly into the page rather than through a 'back-end' content management system. As a result, the barrier to editing is lowered in a way that lowers hassle and so enables more participation.

- Confluence – a nice, hosted (so you don't have to fiddle with the tech) wiki that we use at NixonMcInnes.

- Basecamp – excellent project management and collaboration platform developed by the legends at 37Signals; great for virtual teams.
- IBM Lotus Connections – the 800lb gorilla, again an 'activity stream' plus an internal social network aspect that plugs into other Lotus resources.
- Podio – more like Basecamp – oriented towards groups and projects, under the big corporate radar, and with many of the same useful 'flow' features and philosophy.

What tools like this can enable, if underpinned with the right rewards and cultural changes, is greater knowledge-sharing. Less hoarding, more openness. They are also collaborative in their very nature – you start the page just with a name and a short blurb, tomorrow I add a few bullet points, link it to another wiki page, the day after our other colleague shares it with a few people and they also edit and update it. Remember the stuff about 'always in Beta?'; well here it is.

So progressive businesses use wikis and similar platforms to move from a static and controlled, but largely lifeless traditional intranet approach, to a messier, more emergent, more agile wiki approach. They lower overheads, welcome in collaborators, and get things moving faster.

3 CUSTOMER COMMUNITIES

Perhaps the greatest opportunity, and the only of these which is not inward facing, is the development or engagement with online communities of customers.

A customer community can take many shapes and forms. A loosely formed, ad-hoc customer community may be a group of customers commenting on your organization's blog. A well-established customer community may be a dedicated forum full of rich conversations, both customer-to-customer and customer-to-employee and even customer-to-competitor.

We look at some examples shortly that bring these possibilities to life. In the meantime, perhaps it is worth considering the value of such communities.

What would be the value to your organization of:

- An ever-present group of customers you could poll, listen to, test ideas with and gather insights from?
- A community of super-fans and influencers who are naturally motivated to share your news, launches and in doing so create word of mouth buzz?
- An unpaid volunteer workforce motivated to answer other customers' queries and solve problems together for themselves and others?

This is the prize and certainly a real possibility for all organizations. But you don't get something for nothing! Would you prepared to make the following investments:

- Genuinely listen to, and then regularly (but not always) act on, feedback from the community?
- Enter into dialogue, feedback, provide answers to difficult questions?

■ Commit to generating the community over the long
term and patiently nurture it over years with an eye on
the long term?

If so, technology can provide the platforms to do all of
this. Forums, in particular, are the bedrock of the social web,
kind of like coral reefs, and whilst not particularly glamorous are the teeming ecosystems of communities online.

The technology benefits by not being glamorous: this
is very straightforward stuff, and has been tested and developed over decades. No cutting-edge faff here – just good
solid technology.

The real challenge for you and your organization in
developing a customer community will be in developing the
community. That requires patience and human nurturing.
Community management has become a recognized discipline, and rightly so – it is a vital job, and creates tangible
long-term value. A good community manager is like a good
pub landlord: friendly, welcoming, a natural connector, an
organizer of events that bring the community together, and
willing to play bouncer too – kicking out the bad guys!

So, progressive businesses develop powerful, valuable
customer communities over years. They invest in the community management rather than the technology, and gain
insight, word-of-mouth and lower their costs of marketing
and customer service in doing so.

4   ROLE OF IT

Now to discuss the role of IT! Perhaps you have a wry smile
on your face now, perhaps not. In case it wasn't already clear,

I love technology and the possibilities it creates. What I don't love is the role that many IT departments have played in many organizations. Sorry, IT readers – you are the good guys I'm sure. But seriously, the power went to many of your colleagues' heads. Over and over again I hear from clients in other business functions who tell me that IT are seen as an obstructive and patronizing technology police force.

In these game-changing organizations, we need the best IT people to come to the fore. We need enabling, we need possibilities, we need solutions (not problems! Ahem).

The role of IT and technologists has never been more strategically important. But we need help, not hindrance. Help us understand your challenges openly, like security – a massive god-awful nightmare. And understand our challenges.

Also: help us get under the radar. Take some risks. Leave the navy and join us pirates. We need to get stuff done, bend (or even better, change) some rules!

So which organizations are leading the way?

GIFFGAFF

GiffGaff is an interesting little business that is part of the much bigger O2, which itself is part of the even bigger Telefonica Group. (O2 is the second-largest mobile telecommunications provider in the UK, and now offers internet and financial services too; Telefonica is a Spanish business and currently the world's third largest mobile operator.) GiffGaff is a mobile service provider, and operates as a Mobile Virtual Network Operator on its parent

O2's network. That means GiffGaff acts and behaves as an independent mobile brand, but using the mobile masts, cables and facilities of the O2 network.

GiffGaff, which launched in November 2009 and takes its name from the Scottish Gaelic giffgaff meaning 'mutual giving', brings customers into the heart of its business through technology, primarily through its website. At Giff-Gaff customers are more than just the consumers – they:

- Solve one another's customer service problems through the company's busy forums, only supported by a tiny customer service team.
- Promote GiffGaff to friends through a referral scheme.
- And in doing both of the above, earning virtual 'payback' which can be then converted into airtime, cash or charitable donations.
- Contribute to marketing by developing promotional videos and customer smartphone apps.
- Help select future products and services through their 'Labs', which is effectively a Beta testing approach to new product development.

This isn't just marketing hype. This little division walks the talk: in December 2011 the community 'payback' purse totalled over £700,000 and in the busy customer forums you can find community members whose contributions have totalled many thousands of posts (in a forum a post is a response, like a tweet is to Twitter), totting up lots of kudos and payback points from other GiffGaff customers.

So, what is the point of GiffGaff? What can we take from it? I think there are three standout contributions that GiffGaff makes for its parents and itself:

First, seen from its parent O2's perspective, GiffGaff is an incredible testbed and source of learning and experimentation about how a new kind of tech-enabled approach to mobile phone provision can work. These are approaches to business that would be riskier and also confusing if delivered through the main brand. Instead, here, at arm's length from its parent, GiffGaff can prototype, and boldly play with a very different business model.

Second, by sharing many tasks – like sales, marketing and customer service with customers – GiffGaff lowers costs which can then be passed on to a particular segment of customers who accept that kind of service and seek out that kind of price. That peer-to-peer customer support in particular, delivered through a simple online forum, cuts big costs by avoiding call centres.

Third, the 'Labs' approach through which GiffGaff floats deals and packages for a fixed time period before either dropping them or bringing them into business-as-usual, allows GiffGaff itself to accelerate its own pace of business. This is agile, always-in-Beta thinking in action, and so GiffGaff has a change velocity that is higher than many, if not all, of its competitors.

IBM

At the other end of the spectrum from GiffGaff in terms of business size, global technology giant IBM provides a fine example of walking the talk and, in doing so, demonstrating how a 'social business' (remember the definition from earlier?) can employ technology to create advantage at scale.

The company has:

- SocialBlue – a Facebook-like employee social network – with 53,000 members.
- 17,000 internal blogs, used by some 100,000 employees.
- Multi-day IBM Jam collaboration events involving tens of thousands of internal and external collaborators.

Whereas we looked at GiffGaff's approach to technology through the lens of external collaboration, we can look at IBM's endeavours through an internal collaboration lens.

For starters, given that one of the biggest challenges working in a global corporation is knowing who to speak to about a given issue, a platform like SocialBlue provides both a flow tool, with its activity stream where people can see what other people are up to, but also the social networking equivalent of a telephone directory to help locate and connect with potential collaborators across the company's many geographical locations and business divisions.

There is also the issue of knowledge as power in organizations. This is not a small issue! Knowledge was power, and many people in organizations have responded to this by building powerful personal fortresses to carefully protect their hard-earned knowledge. But in this new world connectivity is power and platforms like SocialBlue in IBM can help to unlock and spread knowledge, and celebrate and reward those people who do just that with their precious expertise.

Additionally, the very act of providing a resource like SocialBlue to its employees is a powerful signal from the company to its people that it 'gets it' and that the company sees substantial value in these new technologies, behaviours and ways of working. That is hugely invaluable in fuelling a culture of technological DNA, even in a tech company (and believe me the two often do not come together – I work regularly with high-tech companies where the majority of people in the business are not big supporters of technology in the delivery of their work).

Perhaps, most exotic of all, IBM's Jam events take collaboration from an always-on background activity, in the flow tools mode, into a more proactive 'events' mode. A Jam is typically a three-day remote collaboration event where people join in discussions and collaborative online working with a specific goal in mind. The first Jam was in 2003 and, over the three days, some 50,000 IBMers helped redefine the company's core values for the first time in 100 years. Since then there have been Security Jam ('brainstorming global security'!), CovJam in partnership with the City Council in Coventry, UK, and Start Jam for business leaders to explore and evolve the next generation of sustainable business strategies, backed by The Prince of Wales.

ATOS, VW AND THE RISE OF BYO IT

Three other promising signs that the way in which technology gets used in major organizations is shifting both to be more people-centric, and more flow-like.

First, Henry Samuel writes for the *Daily Telegraph* about how the former French finance minister and current CEO of Atos, Thierry Breton, plans to massively cut email in their business:

> 'Breton wants a "zero email" policy to be in place within 18 months, arguing that only 10 per cent of the 200 electronic messages his employees receive per day on average turn out to be useful. Instead he wants them to use an instant messaging and a Facebook-style interface.'
> **Amen Monsieur Breton!**

Second, this positive movement grows in momentum – only a few weeks later the works council at VW succeeded in getting VW management to limit emails sent to 1000 employees corporate BlackBerries to 30 minutes before and after their designated shifts. Whilst this may not affect many executives in VW, it still looks like an early outlier to me of a broader push back against some of the expectations that have developed around corporate email and BlackBerries in particular. Contrasted with the *NYT*'s David Carr on how he dips his cup into the river of Twitter updates, email has become the bad-side of always-on – both pervasive and with expectations (and even legal responsibilities) to act on or reply.

Third, perhaps a less controversial but still positive emerging trend in how IT is shifting to enable people in organizations rather than 'manage' them, there is a growing movement towards 'bring your own' technology at work.

As Verne G. Kopytoff writes in the *New York Times* in 2011:

> 'At Kraft Foods, the IT department's involvement in choosing technology for employees is limited to handing out a stipend. Employees use the money to buy whatever laptop they want from Best Buy, Amazon.com or the local Apple store.'

AND THE REST

And of course we've already looked at examples like HCLT, Innocentive, Zappos, Anonymous and Skittles who have all used technology to their distinct advantage both internally and externally.

HOW CAN WE CULTIVATE OUR TECH DNA?

OPENNESS CHANGES EVERYTHING

Fundamentally, the biggest advantages that are gained by pioneering organizations harnessing the power of technology have been covered in Chapter Five: Organizational Openness and – hopefully – reinforced by the examples here.

If you are looking for the game-changing initiative in how technology can substantially propel your business to new heights, I expect openness will be at its core. Crowdsourcing, crowdfunding, open source, APIs, open data –

these terms, these simple words, describe vast, profitable and disruptive seams waiting to be mined. They all involve or are enabled by technology. But, strategically, they are first and foremost about opening up your organization to harness new, previously untapped opportunities.

PEOPLE

Secondly, the only decent way to approach technology in your organization is by adopting a people-first attitude. Fortunately, most entrepreneurs, founders, CFOs and CIOs have learned the hard way that landing a big lump of 'game-changing' technology in the organization and then expecting people to simply fall in love with it then and forever more usually does not work.

To get advantage and value from technology, your people have to approach technology projects by putting users at the heart of everything: the selection, the testing, the management, the training.

Remember what you seek to do: you are changing the culture and developing tech DNA that will positively weave through your company. To enable that, you are applauding progress towards that – especially people changing their own attitudes and overcoming their own fears.

For senior management in large organizations this is especially true. Walking the talk is key. Espousing the supposed benefits and gains that a corporation gets from its latest 'socializing the enterprise' initiative is easy: that confidence and belief in the rest of the organization is somewhat undone when the grapevine reports that the CEO still has his or her assistant 'print off the internet'.

Through user experience (UX)

Activity in brief
Put UX people in charge of important tech projects.

Description
The user experience community has a great deal to offer here. Though these guys are often left to late or worse, never in an internal technology project, they should be right there at the start – hell, they should run the thing. The UX belief system is based on the premise that there is no such thing as a dumb user: the user is right. If you compare that with the IT insider's acronym of RTFM (read the fucking manual) then you can understand why a bit more UX thinking helps internal technology investments generate a much higher return on investment.

Through rewards

Activity in brief
Reward people for thinking and doing technology.

Description
To nurture that digital and technological DNA, you need to reward it in your people. You need to reward non-technical people conceiving of and developing innovations in their area that have a tech element. You need to reward your tech people for finding non-

technical people with business needs that can benefit from technological enablement. You need to celebrate both of these publicly and privately, pay them more, link such behaviour to bonuses, and continuously remind your people of the advantages that come from putting technology at the heart of what you do.

Through role models

Activity in brief
Find positive role models and celebrate them, get existing role models and help them get going.

Description
This role-modelling counts for everyone: the leadership behaviour you are looking for here can come from any part of your team or organization. Leadership in this context is when individuals step up, gather people into a group around an opportunity and issue, transcend any personal history or conventional 'role' they may have in relationship to technology, and helps the organization change.

The flipside is also true. When senior managers really get involved and lead from the front in engaging with technology, the role model provided is irresistible. Powerful examples of visible senior managers using social tools are thankfully many more than they were five years ago. In this book alone we've looked at HCLT (Vineet Nayar engaged in the internal platforms in that organization), Zappos (Tony Hsieh totally gets this stuff, tweets, publishes thoughts, letters, videos on the internet), and you can find many more in each industry and geography. (Oh, and guess what: the visionary leader and the leader that intuitively gets tech are also converging – another prompt for your boss, will they be a dinosaur or a leader among leaders?)

SUMMARY

The world we operate in is increasingly a technologically influenced one. No gold stars for pointing that out. But perhaps we still underestimate just how much technology is changing society, life, our culture and behaviour? Is it by chance that more and more science fiction is based in the present day or just a few years out? We stand with a foot in the past and a foot in the techno-future. The nexus, the inflection point, is right here, today. Has there been a more exciting time to be alive? (Hard to know, right.)

We have a simple choice: to harness the opportunities afforded by that disruption and change, or to resist. From where I stand too many brilliant organizations resist. Perhaps that includes yours. What can you do it about it? The same as every other topic in this book – start something, and show the way.

FURTHER READING

■ 'Structure? The Flatter, the Better', Adam Bryant, *New York Times*, 2010 – includes Conde quote http://nyti.ms/cltrshk9

■ 'Staff to be banned from sending emails', Henry Samuel, *Daily Telegraph*, 2011 – includes Breton quote http://bit.ly/cltrshk10

■ 'More Offices Let Workers Choose Their Own Devices', Verne G. Kopytoff, *New York Times*, 2011 – includes Kraft IT story http://nyti.ms/cltrshk11

■ *Confused of Calcutta* – a brilliant blog by an enlighted, thoughtful technologist JP Rangaswami – http://bit.ly/cltrshk12

■ *Groundswell* by Charlene Li and Josh Bernoff – not new, but still a brilliant overview of the impact and potential of social technologies in organizations

■ Berkman Center for Internet & Society at Harvard University – for articles and insight on digital natives and plenty more http://bit.ly/cltrshk13

■ *Confused of Calcutta* – Stowe Boyd – another excellent blog about the impact of (amongst other things) social tools of business and society – http://stoweboyd.com/

CHAPTER EIGHT

FAIR FINANCES

Before we finish we need to go to what is often seen as the very heart of business – the finances. I am enormously excited about the way that progressive businesses manage their money, and to go on this journey it is vital to get to grips with how the financial aspects of organizations are already evolving and how we can harness those new positive forces.

In the past ten years, the rich got richer and the poor got poorer. And this is happening in some of the most 'developed' nations in the world: according to census data 1 in 15 Americans now rank in the poorest poor – a record high. The tightly interconnected global banking system melted down and it turned out that the regulators and banks themselves didn't know or understand most of what had been going on. At the time of writing the euro currency is standing on a precipice. Politicians continue to be exposed as corrupt. Here in the UK our tax collectors, Her Majesty's Revenue & Customs, have been revealed to have made grossly unfair tax deals with major corporations whilst the poor and at risk suffer the necessary cuts of an Austere Britain, and continue to pay their taxes without the slightest hope of a negotiation with HMRC.

And at the same time, as we have touched on in this book, unpaid armies of volunteers are demonstrating their

power – the Occupy movement, the hacktivists Anonymous, influential communities such as the Wikidians,
the Mumsnetters. These contemporary organizations are
fuelled by meaning more than money.

But still, we need money to live. There is yet to be a
system offered that improves on capitalism. So how can we
mould capitalism and the traditional approaches to money
and finance in organizations to help fuel the organizations
we belong to and believe in? How can we keep the impetus
and energy of capitalism, but make the systems we control
and influence – like how rewards happen in our business,
and how financial performance information is managed –
fairer, more open, more participative? How can we make
our shareholders more resilient and their behaviour more
long-term?

Fortunately, and perhaps not surprisingly, smart, progressive, conscious businesses are doing it for themselves.
They are sticking two fingers up to the conventional wisdom
and finding their own ways to run things in their organizations that others find jaw-dropping. They are handing over
the keys to the company cheque book and credit cards to
anyone in the organization that decides they need them.
They are opening up all of their financial information
including earnings to their whole teams, and sometimes to
the outside world too. They are sharing ownership, rewards
and bonuses far beyond the C-suite. They are the future.

This chapter aims to address the core issue of how to
make the finances of our organizations fairer. Could there
be a more timely issue to immerse ourselves in?

WHY DO PROGRESSIVE APPROACHES TO FINANCE MATTER?

Really simple answer: because the bottom line is that without progressive approaches to finance we're screwed. We, as in present-day society. We, as in citizens, employees, managers, educators, civil servants, parents, passers-by and pensioners (in fact, especially pensioners). We, as in business owners, entrepreneurs, stock holders. In every dimension, we need rapid and urgent shifts in how money gets distributed and handled in the organizations that make up society.

I think there will be bigger changes in the future. Whole system changes. That will be exciting and I don't know about you but I plan on being involved, somehow. But regardless of which doctrine, political system or where on some spectrum you are or what you preferred flavour of the future you'd like to see, it doesn't matter right now – what matters is we substantially evolve things NOW. So we improve what we have. We change towards something bigger and better by starting with this. Here. Now.

Because we need the good stuff that business offers now more than ever. We need a groundswell of small businesses pressing urgently for change, prototyping alternatives and disrupting staid markets and approaches. We need large businesses to deliver large, complex services, to convert large pools of resources into results that benefit society. And how these businesses behave right now, when it comes to money, is screwed.

Fortunately, the prize for fixing them, and being part of the change we want to see in the world, is substantial.

WHAT ARE THE BENEFITS FOR THOSE GRASPING THEM?

Organizations that design progressive financial practices
and systems gain the following benefits:

- Resilience which leads to longer and more stable life-
  spans, from having created stronger, more diverse and
  flexible financial foundations.
- Attraction of talent by promoting their alternatives to
  the practices that so many (especially the best talents)
  have been mistreated by or found wanting.
- Generation of higher profits through unlocking higher
  levels of engagement as a result of greater ownership,
  greater transparency and more positively motivating
  rewards systems.
- Marketing and PR advantage through innovating and
  being able to position themselves against slower-
  to-move alternative providers, and from being the cata-
  lysts that helped their whole financial ecosystem
  (suppliers, employees, customers etc.) implement progressive practices.
- Lower costs, through lower overheads and bureaucracy,
  fewer bottlenecks for financial decisions and greater
  belief in investment and budgeting decisions.

Not on this list, but perhaps most important of all, is
the psychic benefit for having a more positive relationship
with money and the role that it plays in our work. I can't
describe this better than Salman Khan, founder of the
inspiring Khan Academy, which has the stated mission of

'providing a high quality education to anyone, anywhere' (talk about a Purpose of Significance!), and has delivered over 106 million lessons to hundreds of thousands of people since 2006:

> 'When I'm 80, I want to feel that I helped give access to a world-class education to billions of students around the world. Sounds a lot better than starting a business that educates some subset of the developed world that can pay \$19.95/month and eventually selling it to some text book company or something. I already have a beautiful wife, a hilarious son, two Hondas and a decent house. What else does a man need?'

Oh yeah. That too.

WHAT DO FAIR FINANCES LOOK LIKE?

Perhaps the best way to think of this is examine the financial aspects of your (or any business) through the lenses provided by the values that run through this whole book.

Principles like:

- Purpose
- Fairness
- Openness
- Participation
- Resilience

So, let's think about finance from the perspective of each of these Culture Shock values.

PURPOSE

If I ask you what is the purpose of most businesses, what will your answer be? Let's take a wild guess at what your answer might be: to make profits. That's it kids! Take a bow, smile and move to your left – you did *great*. Yet as we looked at in Chapter One: Purpose and Meaning the movers and shakers in the 21st century are driven towards not the creation of profits, but a greater contribution to society. Profits are an important but secondary goal, or even a consequence.

So what is the role of profit in a business motivated to achieving a Purpose of Significance? Fuel.

This next generation of progressive businesses knows well what the fuel of profits bring them. They know that if they are profitable, they can:

- Remain independent and continue to forge their own path, free of parental agenda or alternatively of the huge distraction of raising funding.
- Invest in innovation and continued evolution.
- Attract, reward and retain the best people.
- Distribute profits to an emerging class of enlightened shareholders who can invest again in better businesses.

So know that your future business, or the company you influence today, can move towards a healthier resolution between Purpose in the one hand, and Profit in the other. They can live together. In fact, things work best when they are both present.

But this is not to say that all tension will disappear. There will always be tension between profit and purpose, in my experience. Profit can be hungry and alert in the short term – the profit light blinks on the daily, weekly and monthly dashboard. And profit is a scoreboard – an easy number to track, and so quickly the profit game can create a behaviour in you and those around you who are motivated to win at games.

Purpose, on the other hand, has a slower but possibly greater gravitational pull. Its force is more like a glacier moving than speedboat zigging and zagging of profit. It does not blink on a dashboard, nor is it easy (kind of an understatement) to track in a spreadsheet. Purpose can be found in the gut, in the heart, in the collective wisdom of the people in the organization. So to get that requires 'tuning in' – crucially, you've got to slow down and clear your head to know if you're on or off-purpose. Purpose demands conscience, putting off short-term wins, playing the long game. Purpose tests and torments, lingering in the background, calling you and your organization to strive for more, and provides less of the caffeine-like highs of a profit snack. Given that we are often short-term creatures, is it any wonder why profit can so often overcome purpose?

If you can capture and hold the two in healthy tension, what will that do to your organization? What would it be like to work in a business where both profit and purpose were championed and clearly described?

This is the work we must undertake. There are some suggestions of how to address these issues later in this chapter.

FAIRNESS

Let's start with another question: what is fair or unfair in how mainstream businesses manage their finances? What pops into your mind?

Could it be:

- The balance of the rewards across the organization – especially the difference between those on the frontline and the executives?
- How people doing the same jobs get paid substantially different amounts with no obvious rationale?
- The continued underpaying of women in the workplace?
- The conventional wisdom around managing suppliers, the rise of procurement, and the relationships and dynamics that creates between 'partners'?

Fairness in the context of finance is trickier than it looks at first glance. For example, there is the role of merit. What is fair to one person – who perhaps believes in equal pay across the board for people doing the same role – may feel grossly unfair to another – who may be a high performer who outperforms colleagues in the same role and feels that should be rewarded. Very different views exist in even the most tightly knit little clusters of like-minded people working together. Exposing those differences can be both fascinating and explosive – proceed with care!

To really decide what is 'fair' in some kind of ideological sense we would need to have quite a thorough intellectual discussion and attempt to find a consensus (perhaps using the methods described in Democracy and Empowerment). But putting that to one side for a second, it feels like a societal consensus is emerging at the moment – one which is clearly in contrast with the business-as-usual consensus. Regardless of the intricacies of individuals' views, I am trying to say that a big shift in attitudes is making itself known to us right now. The Occupy movement and the classifications of the 1 per cent and the 99 per cent are early signs that many people, possibly the majority, believe that conventional business is unfair. Put simply: business is seen as a major engine of unfairness.

Imagine if your business could become part of the solution to this and could lead the way by managing finances in a new and agreed 'fair' way. What would that do for you and for your organization? What would it feel like to be a new kind of role model, belonging to a new kind of movement?

So, the sooner we are clear about what we agree in our company is fair, and bring our behaviour into line with it, the sooner we will find ourselves in a sustainable position, able to thrive both now and through changes outside of our control that will come.

OPENNESS

So, how open is your organization when it comes to the finances? Good question eh? Usually brings a smile to the face when asked in a person, particularly I expect in you, being the reader of a book like this. Or a growl, a frown or gasp of horror if it's an old school CFO or accountant! Open?!!

The challenge for those people is that, like it or not, we are hurtling towards a more open world. Open, in that if I find digital information I can share it with millions in minutes. Open, in that culturally and technologically there are shifts towards more open behaviours, systems and attitudes as we looked at in Chapter Five: Organizational Openness.

So where is your organization on this scale:

- Sharing of financial performance with all people in the organization? Daily, weekly, monthly or quarterly?
- Full open book accounting – everyone can find out where every penny goes, including easily finding out what everyone else in the organization earns?
- Transparency of financial performance to the outside world (not through SEC or other stock market requirements)?
- Openly sharing financial metrics twinned with other indicators that matter? E.g. not just share price but share price tracked alongside employee engagement score.

Openness and finance are interesting when paired because they are often so far apart. Certainly in the UK, talking about money and especially personal finances is not something we do well – not like our Dutch, Swedish or German cousins who revel in honesty and directness and will ask questions outright at a dinner party like 'how much do you earn?' But even outside of this little island, businesses have tended to manage their finances like state secrets. Information on a need-to-know basis, layers of authority and access, lots of people kept in the dark, generally very far from transparent – completely opaque, in fact.

Yet, as we explored in Chapter Five: Organizational Openness, there is latent power waiting to be harnessed here. The very energy that is employed to contain the secrecy and opacity around an organization's finances can be converted and multiplied in huge goodwill externally and internally, in saved cost and hassle by freeing the information up and allowing people to employ that energy elsewhere.

PARTICIPATION

Questions to get us started:

- Are the finances and how they are managed a participative activity in your organization?
- To what extent is financial planning and budgeting a team sport? Or is it handled entirely between management and finance?
- Are the rewards structures and shareholding participative – do they welcome in contributions, influence and participation from a broad base or are they reserved for the few?
- What kind of permissions exist for anyone in the organization to make spending or investment decisions? How empowered is the average person in your organization in this context?

As you know, this book (and therefore this author!) believes that this new century will be characterized by participation on a much grander scale and of a much greater significance than has been imagined yet. Participation will imbue everything. People already demand it. And soon it will become unimaginable that I cannot influence your menu, feedback on your product features or help to select our future CEO on platforms that are realtime, open, transparent and participative. So the very same forces will be brought to bear on how businesses manage their finances.

How budgets get set will become more participative (indeed, in Chapter Two we looked at HCLT, and their democratically infused MyBlueprint approach to annual budgeting and business planning). How financial planning, forecasting and business plans get set will become more collaborative. What rewards people in the teams around us receive will become more democratic. Where and how profits are distributed will become more participative. And the results will be tremendous – our organizations will be alive with dialogue, with energized ideas, with healthy conflict. The financial community – management accountants, VP Finances, Finance Directors, CFOs, bookkeepers and the rest – will necessarily shift from being those that know best and keepers of the secrets to curators and managers of community-developed decisions. Their emphasis will shift from 'what to monitor' to 'what to share'.

RESILIENCE

Perhaps easiest to overlook, and hardest to assess, but certainly important is the resilience of how an organization manages its finance. After much environmental, economic and political volatility in the early part of the 21st century, resilience is becoming a more fashionable concept. Read the brilliant best-selling *Black Swan* by Nassim Nicholas Taleb, the excellent *Global Guerillas* blog by John Robb and the writing and events produced by Vinay Gupta. These are all examples of the rise of resilience thinking outside of the security and military communities. But, despite resilience being the new black for some of us, it doesn't seem like everyone wants to take stock of the challenges of the past decade and genuinely fix some of the root causes and, in doing so, make for a more resilient world. We seem to want to hurry on forwards and not really look back.

In finances, there might be a great deal we can do with resilience. By resilience, I mean the ability to withstand challenges, to endure them and to be in a position to continue once they pass (or successfully adapt, if they do not pass).

So useful questions to get thinking about this might be:

- How resilient is your organization financially?
- What gives it financial resilience?
- Where is it not resilient and why?
- Think about: customer relationships, cash reserves, sources of income, ability to find new revenues, fixed cost base, number and strength of relationship with shareholders, reliance on regulation or other forms of protection
- What would your business do to become massively more financially resilient? What would the benefits of that be?

One area that you might have just thought of is the cash reserves your organization has. Or perhaps you thought about risky over-dependences and single points of failure like one hugely valuable customer relationship, or a single dependence on a supplier for key components or services. These all contribute to financial resilience. Perhaps you thought about the shareholders of your business – who are they, is the risk spread widely enough or are there just one or two of them, what is their behaviour likely to be in crisis?

In general, when it comes to financial resilience, small, tightly connected, homogenous groups might not be safe – think global banking system, monocultures in agriculture, or in small businesses, the typically one or two founding shareholders that own the whole show, the folklore about companies that went under because they had one over-arching customer relationship, or NGOs that depended on a single source of funding which had been renewed every year until now. You should also consider the challenges and opportunities laid out in Fairness above: unfair approaches will be increasingly and dramatically less resilient.

OK, so having introduced the principles and ethos of how social businesses approach their finances, let's get practical.

HOW CAN OUR ORGANIZATION WORK TOWARDS FAIRER FINANCES?

There are three categories of opportunities of practical activities – each fits into one of the either Fair Access, Fair Rewards or Fair Influence. Access is probably easiest (although definitely not easy!) to start with, working right up to some of the deeply exciting and powerful possibilities available in Fair Influence which go to the heart of how your organization behaves.

The practical activities

1 Open book accounting (Fair Access)
2 People-powered profit share (Fair Rewards)
3 Ratios between top and bottom (Fair Rewards)
4 Measuring money and happiness (Fair Rewards)
5 Collective budgeting (Fair Influence)
6 Financial empowerment (Fair Influence)
7 Employee ownership (Fair Influence)
8 Fanfunding (Fair Influence)

1 Open book accounting (Fair Access)

Activity in brief
Open up all financial information to the whole organization, and work to develop greater financial literacy in every employee.

Description
Open book accounting is very very simple to implement. You open up the organization's finances, wholly, to everyone inside the organization. Simple. So the challenge or sticking points will not be the practical – they will be cultural, about worldview, perceived wisdom and the 'way things have always been done'.

In our company our Finance Director prepares the monthly management accounts in advance of the board meeting, and in there is the P&L, Balance Sheet, a summary sheet with KPIs (like profit per person), a few other bits and pieces (you expect me to read it all?!) and most importantly her narrative of how the company is doing. And then, quite simply, instead of emailing it to the board, she emails it to the whole team.

Additionally, we have weekly data which is put on the whiteboard for each Monday's whole company (we are 20 or so consultants) weekly stand up: rolling revenue and profit figures for the current and next two months, and team happiness % for the previous week.

At the cardboard box making factory Atlas Container which first led me to find out about Ricard Semler and Semco they taught employees how to read the books. Here's an excerpt from the Inc. article 'The Power of Listening', which I recommend you read in full (see Further Reading):

> 'Employees took in-house classes to learn basic financial concepts. The company began showing them the real numbers – sales, costs, profits, and so on – along with virtually every other piece of information they might want to know. At regular employee meetings the numbers are reviewed and results are forecast.'

So these guys in the competitive corrugated box market can do it – the real question is: what is stopping you/them from opening up the books? And is that barrier fair and is it sustainable, as this movement grows and grows and the world changes around us? Most importantly, have you/they really thought about the benefits of opening up all financial information? About eliminating all of the misconceptions, clearing out some skeletons from the cupboard, empowering people to make decisions and be responsible, having been treated like adults?

2 People-powered profit share (Fair Rewards)

Activity in brief
Give responsibility to employees to influence their colleagues' bonuses.

Description
In many businesses, there is some form of profit-share or bonus scheme. Whilst this sharing of rewards should be applauded – I know I clap loudly every time someone gives me a bonus – there is a feeling sometimes that the calculation on bonuses can be overly opaque, based on the whims or preferences of a few managers. Acknowledging those limitations, companies in this new wave are pioneering new approaches to how such profit schemes are apportioned.

Mint is a much-loved small British company that builds 'delightful social websites' for clients like MTV,

Channel 4, BBC and Sony Ericsson from its London and New York studios. In addition to a variety of other cool contemporary approaches to their business (their WebApp Weekender is a great in-house hackday initiative also worth taking inspiration from), Mint wanted to experiment with an alternative approach to an annual bonus scheme.

Inspired themselves by an earlier effort by another company called Love Machine, Mint decided to do the following in Christmas 2010:

- Give everyone the same amount
- Of which 50% had to be given to other people in the company
- As a result, everyone got the minimum 50%, and then some people got more according to contributions from their peers

As Andy Bell, Mint's Chief Creative Officer recounts in a blog post announcing the scheme and its results:

'1. First and foremost, it has been good fun. It feels powerful and inspiring. It seems to be one of the most popular ideas we've ever tried at Mint. Typical feedback has been along these lines:
'It's a nice opportunity to reward people who've been extra helpful.'
'I really like the idea of the bonus scheme and think this is a great way to divide up the bonus pool.'

2. The most common strategy has been to split the bonus equally across all staff. This seems to be especially true of the people, such as those above, who are big fans of the scheme.

3. In general, we found similar results to those described by LoveMachine. In particular, the system rewarded 'behind-the-scenes' staff over managers. It helped highlight some unsung heroes within Mint.'

For those who feel that such a quirky idea can only live in a small business, check out what IGN Entertainment – a division of the News Corp empire – does with their 'Viral Pay' bonus scheme. Again, the basic principle is of entrusting peers to distribute and influence how the people around them are rewarded. At IGN their twice-yearly 'Viral Pay' scheme has employees use 'Tokens of Appreciation' to share out rewards amongst the company.

In an article in *Fast Company*, Greg Silva, IGN's vice president of People and Places described the origins of the scheme: 'Our employees were saying "It's great that the managers know who's super-effective and contributing the most, but, quite frankly, we know better, so let us reward and recognize our peers."' See Further Reading for a link to the full article.

What do you think? Is there a way you can implement this concept (or a new twist on it) in your team, division or whole organization?

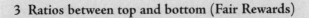

3 Ratios between top and bottom (Fair Rewards)

Activity in brief

Calculate the ratio between the highest paid person in the organization and the lowest paid person, publish it, and create a conversation internally about what ratios should exist.

Description

If we take one thing from the protests, volatility and changes in recent Western society such as the Occupy movement, London riots, and the excellent Gates-Buffett pledge which is successfully encouraging American billionaires to donate 50% or more of their wealth to charity, let it be this: that a yawning schism between the haves and the have-nots is not sustainable. (That it isn't fair is both obvious and also a distracting and potentially long-winded conversation – so for the sake of getting on with things, let's stick to 'unsustainable'.)

Enlightened businesses in our movement have long understood this and have used simple ratios to keep a healthy relationship between the earnings inside their organization to create a haves and also-haves rather than a haves and have-nots.

At Mondragon, the enormously successful Spanish, employee-owned conglomerate whose 250 odd businesses turn over in excess of €14bn annually, a democratic vote within each individual company agrees what the ratio will be between the general manager and executives and those on the frontline. At Mondragon the ratios vary from 3:1 to 9:1, and the average is 5:1 according to Wikipedia (!!). The John Lewis Partnership's constitution says 'The pay of the highest-paid partner will be no more than 75 times the average base pay of non-management partners on an hourly basis'. So that's 75:1 – not bad! And staying in the UK, according to an article from the Chartered Institute of Personal Development, Will Hutton, the writer and champion of fairness, has been asked if a ratio of 20:1 in public sector pay will 'promote fairness'. When we last calculated mine in May 2010 my pay was 2.1 times the average salary in the rest of the team. Plenty of headroom for a payrise I reckon!

It seems the ratios themselves are flexible and can work effectively according to the particular organization, its desires, purpose, constitution and business dynamics. But the principle is what is powerful – that there is a conscious and clear link created and monitored between the rewards of those at the grassroots and those at the lofty heights. This will only grow. Get ahead.

4 Measuring money and happiness (Fair Rewards)

Activity in brief

Implement Happy Buckets, and start including happiness measures alongside all financial and operational reports to provide important context on how well the organization is doing from a holistic perspective.

Description
One of the issues business has with how it manages its financial affairs has been the addictive quality of purely financial measures: their absoluteness, their simplicity, their clarity. Unfortunately, as we seem to be realizing, those measures do not capture everything that matters – much like that famous line from Oscar Wilde: 'A man who knows the price of everything, and the value of nothing'.

As a result, in both society and in individual organizations, I believe we will see more and more classical metrics twinned with happiness, well-being, purpose or other 'meaning' measures that bring some much-needed missing human and real-world context to otherwise cold, inert figures.

So in your business, why not implement the Happy Buckets practice described in Chapter Three: Progressive People? Then begin including the happiness measures in the relevant financial and operational reports. In doing so, you will create a new understanding of the fairness of rewards.

If happiness is bombing, but profit is flying, reporting the two data points in the same breath will prevent people from zeroing in on one at the expense of the other. To quote Peter Drucker again: 'what gets measured gets managed'. If you encourage the

measurement of happiness in your business in relationship to financial performance you will help the
organization better manage both aspects of the
organization's performance and see them as in relation with one another rather than entirely divorced.

5 Collective budgeting (Fair Influence)

Activity in brief
Create platforms or processes to allow full and un-
precedented access to company budgeting and planning including voting on which investments the
company should prioritize in the period.

Description
In Democracy and Empowerment we saw how
HCLT, the rapidly growing Indian software business,
had created a powerful cultural shift by implementing
a number of processes and platforms that celebrated
the contributions of people across the whole organization, from the grassroots up. If we take that ethos
and apply it to budgeting and planning, isn't there
more we could all be doing in involving our people
– the people who will actually deliver the results?

   At NixonMcInnes we follow a fairly standard
approach to budgeting: each manager puts together
a plan for their area for the coming year; the FD
aggregates each piece of the jigsaw; and then, as
things start coming together, talks to a few directors

about what the whole plan looks like and where things are out of kilter. Nothing new here.

Our only democratic twist in the last financial year was that when we got to a point where every initiative, investment and area was in relative balance it became clear that we could not do everything we wanted to in the year. Some stuff had to give – in fact, quite a lot had to give. The board failed to find the areas to de-prioritize, and so it fell to the team. We held a company-wide 'team budgeting session'. With hindsight 'gladatorial bloodbathing session' would have been a better name. But you know what? The team did what the board could not. They made the budget work.

As a result we had a company-wide understanding of what the annual plan and budget comprised of, a good handle on the rationales and expected outcomes from the investments in each area, and a deeper level of engagement in the team (although many will still shake their heads if you ever get a chance to ask them about the 'budgeting session' – it really was ugly and badly managed for which I take full responsibility).

In a more organized, thought-out environment, what could this concept of collective budgeting become?

What I would like to see, and what is possible in some of your organizations for sure, is a Kickstarter-esque approach to annual planning. Kickstarter, as described in Chapter Five: Organizational Openness, is the crowdfunding platform that allows people to get their creative projects funded. So why wouldn't a large progressive organization, with a good or developing Techn DNA, manage an annual budgeting process using a Kickstarter-like platform where employees can help the organization whittle down a long-list of potential investments for the year ahead, and then put their vote/token/budget towards the investments they believe should be shortlisted? I'm sure that in the next ten years this will become common and established practice in progressive organizations.

6 Financial empowerment (Fair Influence)

Activity in brief
Substantially increase the authority of everyone in the organization to make financial decisions.

Description
At Semco, anyone can make any kind of financial decision. They trust people to make the right decisions. That's it. Done.

I will never forget (I say that, but actually I have a terrible memory after being knocked out playing rugby a few years ago) how Semler describes the story of a regular guy in a division hiring a private helicopter on a company credit card, with no permission, to fly a high-value potential client around a particular site. Of course, it was the right decision, the deal was won, and with hindsight that kind of financial freedom made absolute sense.

Semco do this because they believe that people are smart, that they can trust their people to make good decisions (and do every day elsewhere in the business, so why not with finances?) and because it helps to get things done.

The questions for you are:

- Can you make this happen at your work?
- What's a step that you can take in the right direction?
- Who do you need to bring with you?
- What is your/their greatest fear and how can it be mitigated?

7 Employee ownership (Fair Influence)

Activity in brief
Assess and implement one of the many approaches that allow employees to become owners of the company.

Description
Employee ownership is a fairly rich area. Which is a nice way of saying that there are a number of different flavours and approaches to employee ownership, each with their own supporters and nuances. So, in this book, we will stay high level, and point you to other resources where – once you're motivated – you will find out more.

For me, employee ownership is *the* single most powerful lever available in the whole of *Culture Shock*. And I say that from a perspective of intuitively believing rather than knowing first-hand, because NixonMcInnes has plans to increase employee ownership and has carried out extensive investigations and planning, but has not yet made it happen. Terms and conditions apply, the value of your investment may go down as well as up, caveat, caveat, caveat. But, disclaimers aside, I believe that everything that this book strives to achieve can be partially or wholly achieved through shifting to or starting from a basis of employee ownership.

Employee ownership structures vary. The Employee Ownership Association in the UK describes these as:

- Direct employee ownership – using one or more tax advantaged share plans, employees become registered individual shareholders of a majority of the shares in their company.
- Indirect employee ownership – shares are held collectively on behalf of employees, normally through an employee trust.
- Combined direct and indirect ownership – a combination of individual and collective share ownership.

Regardless of structure, from talking to people I have found that quite understandably most people think 'employee ownership' means 'co-operative', so please know this: a co-operative is just one form of employee ownership. Co-operative comes with a particular set of conditions, expectations and approaches.

There are many others, but it really depends on your national laws and available frameworks – in the US the ESOP (Employee Share Ownership Plans) are a widely understood and widely distributed scheme. Importantly, ESOPs are both entrepreneur- and employee-friendly. In the UK there is a growing fondness of 'mutuals' from the current government, so we hope to see some helpful changes here that will see a whole generation of employee-owned businesses bloom. But, whatever the case, know that picking your flavour of structure is part of the process, and you can find a type that suits your situation and goals.

The prize of creating real employee ownership is tangible, cultural and behavioural and has been proven through a number of rigorous academic studies including Cass Business School. Imagine if all of the people around you actually *owned* the organization you work for. If you're a manager, imagine how that would shift your relationship, the scrutiny of your performance, that extra last few % of care, attention and love that your people would put into their work, the challenges they would pose to strategy and senior management decision-making.

If you are an entrepreneur, imagine if you could harness the total and utter commitment to the cause from every person that joins your new or growing enterprise. Imagine the edge you could gain by telling potential clients about the quality of service that they will get by being handled by owners, and imagine the talent you could attract and retain.

Well-known successful businesses which are employee-owned include:

- Arup – UK, world renowned engineering consultancy with 92 offices worldwide and £800m annual turnover.
- John Lewis Partnership – UK, Britain's much loved and hugely successful retailing group with 76,000 employees.
- Mondragon Corporation – Spain, turnover of some €14bn and operates over 250 companies.
- Publix Supermarket – USA, rapidly growing and already employing over 150,000 employees.
- W. L. Gore – yep, them again!

8 Fanfunding (Fair Influence)

Activity in brief

Raise finance and extend ownership to your customers and fans.

Description

In this book we have looked at how this new wave of progressive businesses is opening up its edges, creating a more porous flow of information, ideas and effort between their interiors and the outside world. What would that trend look like applied to finance?

Consider the case of BrewDog. An independent brewer of craft beer, BrewDog was set up in 2007 by two Scottish friends James and Martin and now makes hundreds of thousands of bottles of beer a month which are exported globally and sold from their growing BrewDog bar chain both in Scotland and England. Although the business is financially successful, with a turnover of some £6.5m in 2011, it is also capital-intensive: you need big lumps of cash to pay for the land, buildings and equipment necessary to grow. Cue Equity for Punks I and II.

In 2009 the BrewDog guys needed to raise some money to continue growing, so they came up with Equity for Punks – an 'online IPO' to allow fans and the wider general public to buy shares in the company. They raised the money from over 1000 new investors. Crucially, it isn't just a straight financial offer – the whole positioning, the benefits and even the name of Equity for Punks make it clear this is more than just raising funds (which is frankly quite boring). This is about creating something bigger. It is about strengthening the relationship between the beer drinker and the beer producer – benefits of becoming a shareholder include the straight stuff (come to the AGM), and the alcoholic stuff (get discounts off our beer, hear news from us regularly).

This time round, Equity for Punks II, the guys wanted to raise more cash – here's why in their own words:

'We want to build a hardcore eco brewery just outside
Aberdeen to enable us to keep up with demand for
our beers and help us continue our mission to make
other people as passionate about great craft beer as we
are. The new facility will give our business amazing
growth potential, enabling us to continue our strong
growth as well as continuing to build the value of your
investment. We also want to bring you more places to
enjoy great beer. With each new bar we establish a
stronghold for the craft beer revolution. Our new
bars will showcase BrewDog beers as well as bringing
you some of the most sought after craft beers from all
corners of the planet.'

Already they've raised over £1.7m from more than
5000 investors. And one of them is me! Funnily
enough, but perhaps not unusually, I liked the
approach so much that I just had to join the gang; I
wanted to be part of it. Only then did I notice their
Punk IPA beer in a supermarket and became a customer (now my favourite beer – small tins, lovely flavours, ridiculously strong). But that total relationship
of investor and customer feels really strong. I want to
see them succeed and I feel part of it.

We've talked about crowdfunding, about Kickstarter, and about the wider concepts of participation
and openness. In this example, BrewDog shows us
the other end of that spectrum – raising millions to
spend on heavyweight, tangible, industrial business-y

stuff. And I am sure we will see significant growth in these kind of financings which are part financial, part community, part marketing. So how can you employ this practice in your organization? What's coming up that you could flip on its head and both raise money and awareness?

SUMMARY

Isn't it incredible that we can find such exciting, inspiring innovation in the area of finance, the area often talked down as bean counting and the holder of the status quo? But it really doesn't need to be like this, as I hope this chapter shows. Powerful change is happening at the intersection of progressive business and finance. New tools and approaches are emerging and gaining in momentum, while other long-established (like employee ownership) seem to be finding a new gear.

What's more, the benefit of working on the financial aspects of the organizations we work in and help create is that we are working at the core. The money stuff is what makes so much of business tick – rightly or wrongly – and by tweaking those mechanisms, those measures, we can change the whole machine. As I write this, I'm thinking of 20th century business as a human being, with a human heart, and hands and eyes, arms and legs, but peel back the skin and underneath there was a giant clockwork machine. It should have been human, it kinda looked human, but the way it worked was mechanical, and it took over. The heart withered, the eyes glazed over, but that internal ticking kept turning over, counting the profits, measuring, monitoring, squeezing more. In the 21st century, business will become more human, it will become an organism again, and we will keep the good bits of the well-oiled machine, but we need everything – including our finances – to be people-centred, to have heart, and to be helping to make a positive difference. Thanks for listening.

FURTHER READING

■ 'The Power of Listening', John Case, *Inc. Magazine*, 2003 – the article that led NixonMcInnes to become a democratic business, includes examples of training a manufacturing workforce in financial concepts and regularly sharing financial information http://bit.ly/cltrshk4

■ 'The Rewarder', Andy Bell, *Mint Digital*, 2010 – blog post detailing Mint's innovative people-powered bonus scheme http://bit.ly/cltrshk14

■ 'At IGN, Employees Use A "Viral Pay" System To Determine Each Others' Bonuses', E.B. Boyd, *Fast Company*, 2011 – http://bit.ly/cltrshk15

■ Cass Business School study into performance of employee-owned businesses – http://bit.ly/cltrshk16

CONCLUSION

So you got here! We are nearly done.

In getting to the end of this book, you've experienced and understood how a new wave of businesses is doing things differently. And perhaps you yourself have been on a mini-journey in the way that we do when we read books. Perhaps there have been moments when you have smiled with delight, frowned in contemplation, shaken your head in resistance, and felt little flickers of adrenaline at the possibilities that exist for you and your organization. Maybe you made detailed notes, or maybe you dreamed big. Maybe you just plodded through it! But something – I hope – has changed in you.

In writing this, the goal was to provide not only the inspiration and belief, but also to help you by stimulating practical actions and real-world next steps.

To help make this movement both comprehensible and then in some way actionable we broke the major components of progressive businesses down into practical chapters:

- Purpose and Meaning
- Democracy and Empowerment
- Progressive People
- Conscious Leadership

- Organizational Openness
- Change Velocity
- Tech DNA
- Fair Finances

Can you remember the sections that resonated most for you and your situation? Go back to these. Remind yourself of the opportunities available there.

These are the levers for you to pull, the areas for you and your team to focus in on. In each given area there is a substantial opportunity to make a difference to how your existing or future organization behaves. And as you now know, they overlap hugely – to separate them into satisfyingly distinct individual parts is really just a necessity to make the book work. This is all one big thing – a feeling, a movement, a tribe, a new way.

What will it be like when you start taking action, if you haven't already? It will be hard. I know from my own personal experience that taking an alternative path isn't the easy approach. The world is geared up for Route 1 – business 101, the way it's always been done. In taking this alternative you will hit barriers.

That said, the benefits are immeasurable. Both organizationally and individually you will:

- Be more flexible and resilient as the world changes around you.
- Become truly different as an organization, which will help you stand out from me-too competitors.

- Learn how to lead in a changed world.
- Attract incredible people, partners and collaborators to your team and wider organization.
- Innovate faster, better and at lower cost.
- Make better decisions, which will lead to greater success however you define that.
- Gain the fulfilment and deep satisfaction that comes with doing things that right way.
- Be part of the solution rather than the problem.

WHAT NOW?

You know what really matters now: action.

We have no time to lose. This is not about me or you or a cosy club of likeminded 'visionary' entrepreneurs. It is not only about creativity or profits or better outcomes. It is about the future of the world. I know that is ridiculous: I'm British – it is not customary to talk in such grandiose terms. But really, it is.

What is the alternative? Watch the fools currently running things continue to melt the world down and stash it in Swiss bank accounts? Sit and wait for some kind of imminent but non-specific 'whole paradigm' shift? Pretend nothing is going wrong and diligently behave like a good consumer-worker-drone – eating, sleeping, watching TV and keeping your head down between 9 am and 5 pm? Or, perhaps worst of all, sit back and point the finger at 'them' – those that have got us it in to this terrible mess? Nope. Not good enough. Not meaningful enough. Not empowered enough.

That is not the way for us. We must take action. We must be part of the solution. We must be the change we want to see in the world. If we take action, today, we can collectively make this world better.

I can imagine a world in 20 years' time where people work together better, create better results that have meaning and worth in the world, share in decisions that affect them at work and in life, and share in the rewards that flow from that work. (In some places, that happens today.)

I can imagine a world in 20 years' time where leadership is defined by followership, where listening, empathy, dialogue and authenticity are sought-after CEO traits, where leadership permeates whole organizations, and where individuals and organizations adapt constantly in response to the world around them. (In some places, that too happens today).

I can imagine a world where you and I and he and she can all look back and say 'can you believe it was really like *that* back then?' A place where we can stand up and say that we were part of something that made the world better, that we took a different path, that we fought, and struggled, and persisted, and led ourselves and others to the higher ground.

If you can imagine that future world too, take action. START NOW!

Will McInnes
@willmcinnes
http://www.nixonmcinnes.co.uk/
http://willmcinnes.com/

ACKNOWLEDGEMENTS

All that I know and share in this book came from others and the world around me. I am just the messenger. So, my acknowledgements can never really capture it all, but I'll give it a go.

I am very grateful to my teammates. You mean so much to me. You are the most talented, brilliant, good-hearted and real bunch of people and to work with you every day is a privilege. Thank you!

Tom Nixon was a brilliant business partner – we had an absolute ball, bumbling from startup to creating a consultancy that is now rightly respected and really stands for something. Thank you Tom for your humour, your bulletproof-ness and your willingness to eat curry. Pete Burden has been our sage guide on that journey, my coach who has given so generously his wisdom, his challenge and his support over the years. Thank you Pete – you are a great man and a challenging mentor.

Our company NixonMcInnes has been fortunate to partner with fantastic clients: thank you to you all especially: Channel 4, Cisco, Barclaycard, Barclays, Foreign & Commonwealth Office, Juniper, Nectar, RSPCA, Telefonica O2, Virgin Media and WWF UK.

I must also acknowledge two products that were influential in the creation of this book: namely the music of Sasha and the writing software package Scrivener. I wrote this book in about three months and over those weeks and months the music of Sasha helped me settle into flow day after day, week after week. Nothing else took me to the same place as quickly and smoothly. I literally couldn't have done it without it! And Scrivener is a wonderful piece of software for writing if you want to get away from the tools and baggage that come with your everyday work software.

Most of all, I am grateful each day for the love and support of my family. My mum, for her spirit, her quickness of thought and love. My dad for his generosity with time, his ability to explain and teach, and his belief in me. To my sister, Grace and brother, Louis for being mad awesome lovely crazies. Thank you, Karen, for always believing in me and your unswerving support through thick and thin. You are a beautiful, wonderful woman. And to my two boys for providing meaning, entertainment, warmth and love. You mean everything to me.

Finally, I am very grateful to all those that contributed with comments and additions as I wrote the book. Thank you so much for your time, your intelligence and your efforts – you made the book better and gave me confidence and belief to stay on the path!

THANK YOU
Tim Aldiss
Sam Assefi
Miranda Ash
Tom Bailey
Stuart Bagshaw
Pete Burden
Neil Denny
Andy Fox
Matthew Grenier
Ronan Harrington
Paul Hutchings
Jenni Lloyd
David Lockie
Maria Marzaoli
Antony Mayfield
Tom Nixon
Sarah Ogden
Giles Palmer
Sejal Parekh
Mark Pinsent
Gareth Rackley
Chris Reed
Sarah Rah
Matt Scott

Mark Sears

Jonathan Shipley

Max St. John

Mark Walker

Nathaniel Whitestone

Dan Wilson

Caz Yetman

ABOUT WILL MCINNES

Will McInnes is Managing Director of Nixon-McInnes, co-organiser of progressive business conference Meaning and a passionate voice on 21st century business at events around the world.

After dropping out of university and a brief stint in a conventional job Will started a different kind of company with fellow young entrepreneur Tom Nixon.

NixonMcInnes is now a pioneering social business consultancy working with large organizations that need to change their culture, structure and skills to meet the demands of business in the 21st century. The company has been recognized by WorldBlu as one of the most democratic workplaces in the world for three years running.

Clients have included BBC, Barclays, Channel 4, Cisco, O2, The Foreign & Commonwealth Office and WWF.

Will lives in the creative city of Brighton, UK with his wife and two energetic young sons. He is a mountain biking geek, loves camping in the great outdoors and eating far too much curry.

INDEX